BELL UH~1

Christopher Chant

Foulis

Haynes

ISBN 0 85429 437 6

A FOULIS Aircraft Book

First published 1985

© **Winchmore Publishing Services Limited 1985**

Published by:
Haynes Publishing Group
Sparkford, Yeovil,
Somerset BA22 7JJ

Haynes Publications Inc.
861 Lawrence Drive,
Newbury Park,
California 91320, USA

Produced by:
Winchmore Publishing Services Limited,
40 Triton Square,
London NW1 3HG

Printed in England

British Library Cataloguing in Publication Data

Chant, Christopher
  Bell U-HI super profile.
  1. Bell helicopter
  I. Title
  629.133'352   TL716.9.B4
  ISBN 0-85429-437-6

Also available:
Avro Vulcan (F436)
B29 Superfortress (F339)
Boeing 707 (F356)
De Havilland Mosquito (F422)
Harrier (F357)
Mikoyan-Gurevich MiG 21 (F439)
P51 Mustang (F423)
Phantom II (F376)
Sea King (F377)
SEPECAT Jaguar (F438)
Super Etendard (F378)
Tiger Moth (F421)
Grumman Bearcat F8F (F447)
Hawker Hunter (F448)
Douglas Dakota (F449)
Hercules (F450)
Gloster Meteor (F451)

Further titles in this series will be published at regular intervals. For information on new titles please contact your bookseller or write to the publisher.

Contents

Library of Congress Catalog
Card Number
Bell UH1 84-48558

Genesis

Produced in a number of forms with different one- and two-engine powerplant and with different sizes of fuselage and main rotor, the prolific Bell 'Huey' has been in production for over one-quarter of a century and has been known by a number of names and designations. It is impossible to overrate the signal importance of this classic helicopter, the first turbine-powered utility helicopter to enter large-scale production in the USA: almost single-handedly it transformed the world's opinion of the capabilities of the helicopter, which had in its previous turbine-powered form been a useful but highly limited machine retained more for its unique capabilities than for its versatility and genuine commercial and/or military utility. Since its service debut as a training, utility and casualty evacuation machine, the 'Huey' has been developed quite enormously by its parent company and by various licensees (especially Agusta in Italy) as one of the most versatile aircraft in the world. It should be noted at this stage that during the 1960s this development split into two branches, namely the utility helicopter and the gunship helicopter, and that this survey is limited to the former type as the latter is a much-altered machine worthy of a survey in its own right. The scale of the whole 'Huey' programme, in all its military and civil variants, is indicated by the fact that production has now exceeded 26,000 units, though precise production figures are almost impossible to determine because of the degree of secrecy imposed by Bell Helicopter Textron, the primary manufacturer.

Three-view illustration of the Bell UH-1H with (bottom) a side view of the Bell UH-1A for comparison of the later model's lengthened fuselage.

Key to success of the 'Huey' was the adoption of a turbine rather than reciprocating powerplant. Piston engines had been used in all early helicopters, but had limited the helicopters' capabilities by reason of their relatively low power-to-weight ratios and high volume-to-weight ratios. The latter, combined with the very weight of any piston engine, be it of water-cooled inline or air-cooled radial type (only the latter being used successfully in early helicopters), meant that engines had generally to be placed low in the fuselage for stability purposes, which entailed the use of lengthy (and also heavy) transmission shafts up to a cumbersome and also heavy gearbox mounted close to the rotor assembly. It was a workable arrangement, but it was very far from ideal, especially when the vibration aspects of the reciprocating engine were added to the equation. The turbine offered a relatively simple solution to most of these problems, and this fact was appreciated relatively early in the history of successful helicopter flight. The problem, during the latter half of the 1940s, however, lay with the relative unreliability of turbine powerplants and with such powerplants' high fuel consumption. Rapid strides were made in both fields, and by 1950s the turbine was fast emerging as a formidable powerplant. In the helicopter application it offered singular advantages in comparison with a reciprocating powerplant: it has a high power-to-weight ratio and low volume-to-weight ratio, and is relatively free from coarse vibration. This means that the powerplant can be installed relatively high on the airframe, in most cases above the cabin roof adjacent to the rotor assembly in a position where no transmission shafts are needed, and as well as saving weight this permits a greater part of the airframe to be used for payload purposes. While payload benefits accrue from the smaller volume and lighter weight of the turbine powerplant, these are increased by the turbine's better power-to-

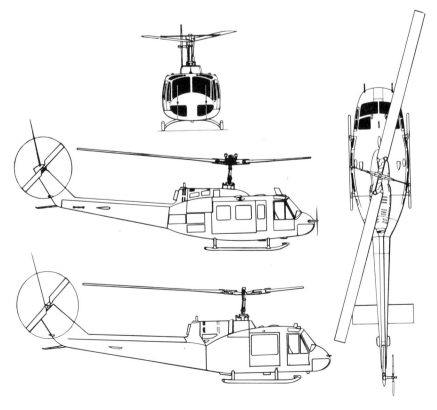

weight ratio at the same time that performance is considerably enhanced in overall terms. It can thus fairly be said that the development of the turbine powerplant completely altered the nature of the helicopter, turning it from a fairly brutish infant into the controlled adolescent that is still making great strides towards a full maturity. The first US helicopter to capitalize on the capabilities of the turbine powerplant in a major way was the 'Huey', the world's first 'workhorse' utility helicopter.

The 'Huey' was not the first turbine-powered US helicopter, however, this honour falling to the Kaman K-225 experimental machine. Bell too had been interested in the potential of turbine power from an early stage (the company had, after all, designed and built the first American turbine-powered

aircraft, the P-59 Airacomet experimental fighter at the end of World War II), this interest being expressed in the XH-13F, an experimental development of the military counterpart of the Model 47 light helicopter with a Continental XT15-T-3 turbine (licence-built Turboméca Artouste). Results of the flight trials were highly encouraging during 1954, though military retrenchment in the aftermath of the Korean War, which had ended in the previous year, prompted Bell not to consider a production variant in an airframe of limited capabilities. (It is interesting to note, though, that some years later the turbine had become so widely accepted that Soloy undertook a programme to re-engine Model 47 light helicopters with a turbine powerplant.)

The experience with the XH-13F

stood the company in good stead when the US Army in 1954 reviewed the nature of helicopter operations in the Korean War and issued a requirement for a new utility helicopter that would be ordered in large numbers. The missions required of the winning design were general utility, the front-line evacuation of casualties, and instrument flying training. The US Army specified a turbine powerplant, and other design requirements were the ability to lift an 800-lb (363-kg) payload over a mission radius of 115 miles (185 km), ease of transport aboard US Air Force freight aircraft, easy field maintainability, and the ability to carry men, supplies and small items of equipment.

The 'Huey' was schemed right from its inception as a casualty-evacuation helicopter in the role seen here.

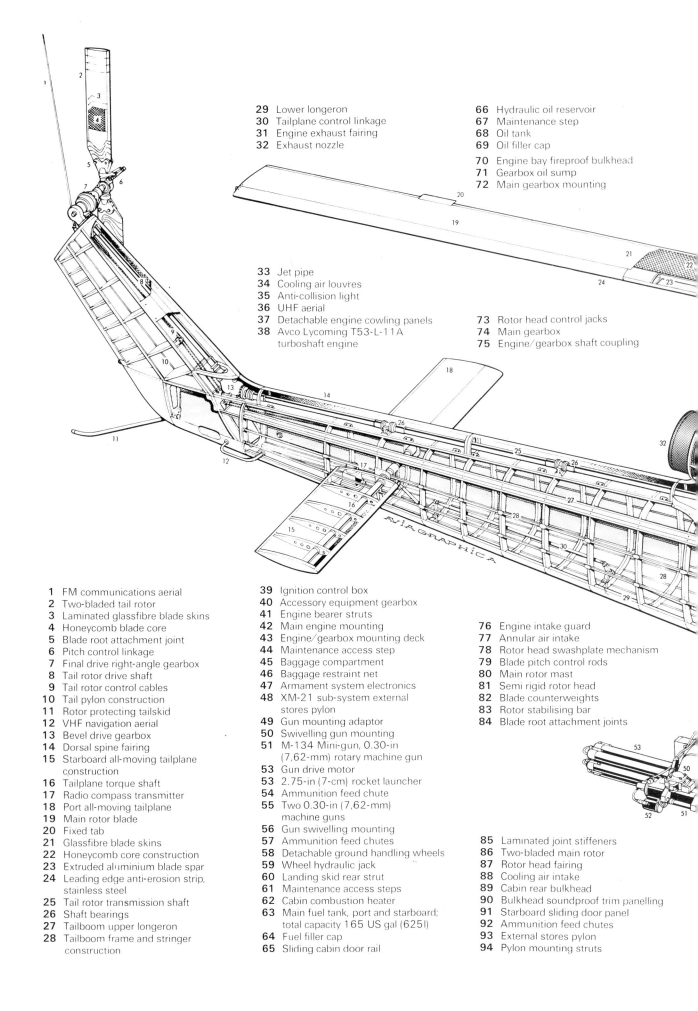

29 Lower longeron
30 Tailplane control linkage
31 Engine exhaust fairing
32 Exhaust nozzle

66 Hydraulic oil reservoir
67 Maintenance step
68 Oil tank
69 Oil filler cap
70 Engine bay fireproof bulkhead
71 Gearbox oil sump
72 Main gearbox mounting

33 Jet pipe
34 Cooling air louvres
35 Anti-collision light
36 UHF aerial
37 Detachable engine cowling panels
38 Avco Lycoming T53-L-11A
   turboshaft engine

73 Rotor head control jacks
74 Main gearbox
75 Engine/gearbox shaft coupling

1 FM communications aerial
2 Two-bladed tail rotor
3 Laminated glassfibre blade skins
4 Honeycomb blade core
5 Blade root attachment joint
6 Pitch control linkage
7 Final drive right-angle gearbox
8 Tail rotor drive shaft
9 Tail rotor control cables
10 Tail pylon construction
11 Rotor protecting tailskid
12 VHF navigation aerial
13 Bevel drive gearbox
14 Dorsal spine fairing
15 Starboard all-moving tailplane
   construction
16 Tailplane torque shaft
17 Radio compass transmitter
18 Port all-moving tailplane
19 Main rotor blade
20 Fixed tab
21 Glassfibre blade skins
22 Honeycomb core construction
23 Extruded aluminium blade spar
24 Leading edge anti-erosion strip,
   stainless steel
25 Tail rotor transmission shaft
26 Shaft bearings
27 Tailboom upper longeron
28 Tailboom frame and stringer
   construction

39 Ignition control box
40 Accessory equipment gearbox
41 Engine bearer struts
42 Main engine mounting
43 Engine/gearbox mounting deck
44 Maintenance access step
45 Baggage compartment
46 Baggage restraint net
47 Armament system electronics
48 XM-21 sub-system external
   stores pylon
49 Gun mounting adaptor
50 Swivelling gun mounting
51 M-134 Mini-gun, 0.30-in
   (7,62-mm) rotary machine gun
53 Gun drive motor
53 2.75-in (7-cm) rocket launcher
54 Ammunition feed chute
55 Two 0.30-in (7,62-mm)
   machine guns
56 Gun swivelling mounting
57 Ammunition feed chutes
58 Detachable ground handling wheels
59 Wheel hydraulic jack
60 Landing skid rear strut
61 Maintenance access steps
62 Cabin combustion heater
63 Main fuel tank, port and starboard;
   total capacity 165 US gal (625l)
64 Fuel filler cap
65 Sliding cabin door rail

76 Engine intake guard
77 Annular air intake
78 Rotor head swashplate mechanism
79 Blade pitch control rods
80 Main rotor mast
81 Semi rigid rotor head
82 Blade counterweights
83 Rotor stabilising bar
84 Blade root attachment joints

85 Laminated joint stiffeners
86 Two-bladed main rotor
87 Rotor head fairing
88 Cooling air intake
89 Cabin rear bulkhead
90 Bulkhead soundproof trim panelling
91 Starboard sliding door panel
92 Ammunition feed chutes
93 External stores pylon
94 Pylon mounting struts

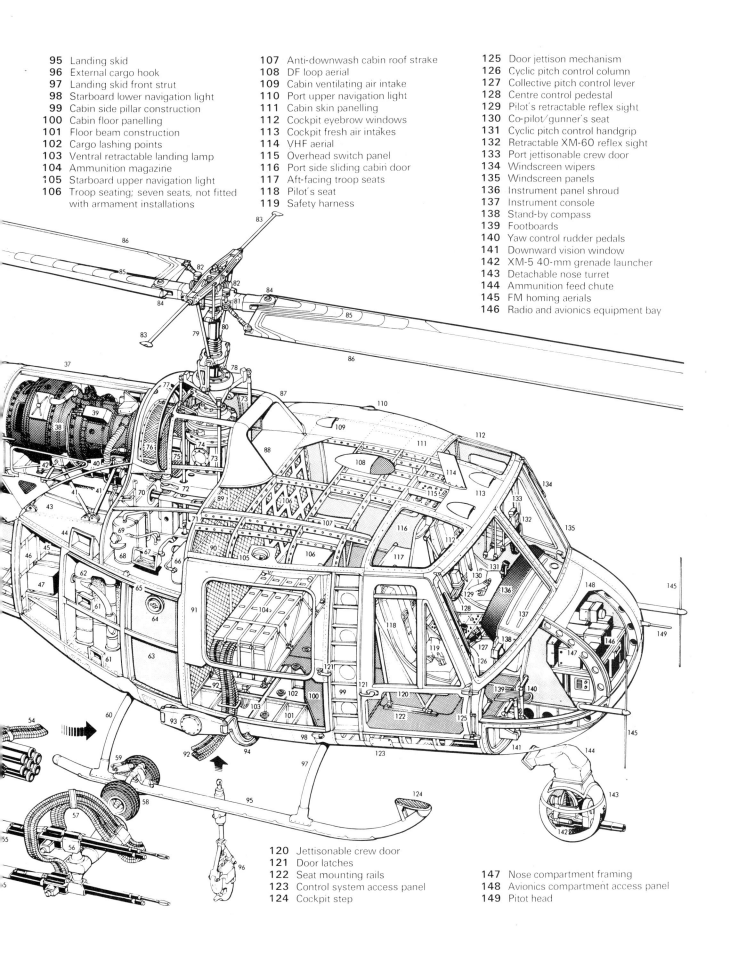

95 Landing skid
96 External cargo hook
97 Landing skid front strut
98 Starboard lower navigation light
99 Cabin side pillar construction
100 Cabin floor panelling
101 Floor beam construction
102 Cargo lashing points
103 Ventral retractable landing lamp
104 Ammunition magazine
105 Starboard upper navigation light
106 Troop seating; seven seats, not fitted
    with armament installations

107 Anti-downwash cabin roof strake
108 DF loop aerial
109 Cabin ventilating air intake
110 Port upper navigation light
111 Cabin skin panelling
112 Cockpit eyebrow windows
113 Cockpit fresh air intakes
114 VHF aerial
115 Overhead switch panel
116 Port side sliding cabin door
117 Aft-facing troop seats
118 Pilot's seat
119 Safety harness

125 Door jettison mechanism
126 Cyclic pitch control column
127 Collective pitch control lever
128 Centre control pedestal
129 Pilot's retractable reflex sight
130 Co-pilot/gunner's seat
131 Cyclic pitch control handgrip
132 Retractable XM-60 reflex sight
133 Port jettisonable crew door
134 Windscreen wipers
135 Windscreen panels
136 Instrument panel shroud
137 Instrument console
138 Stand-by compass
139 Footboards
140 Yaw control rudder pedals
141 Downward vision window
142 XM-5 40-mm grenade launcher
143 Detachable nose turret
144 Ammunition feed chute
145 FM homing aerials
146 Radio and avionics equipment bay

120 Jettisonable crew door
121 Door latches
122 Seat mounting rails
123 Control system access panel
124 Cockpit step

147 Nose compartment framing
148 Avionics compartment access panel
149 Pitot head

Tenders were received for no fewer than 20 designs, and after an exhaustive evaluation of the competing offers, the US Army in June 1955 announced that the Bell Model 204 submission had been selected as the winner, and that three XH-40 prototypes had been ordered for test and evaluation with the 700-shp (522-kW) Avco Lycoming T53 turboshaft engine.

Construction of the three prototypes moved ahead smoothly, the design being characterized by a tadpole-like fuselage with a bulged forward section for the crew and payload tailing into a relatively slim boom to support the tail rotor assembly. Fuel was located in cells under the floor of the cabin, which was entirely unencumbered by

dynamic-system components, all of which were located above the cabin ceiling in a group round the hub assembly for the two-blade main rotor of typical Bell design. There was nothing exceptional about the design, but all its components blended into a harmonious whole that promised volumes for the eventual success of the basic concept.

The first XH-40 (US Army Serial number 55-4459) flew on 22 October 1956, just two days after the death of Lawrence 'Larry' Bell, the founder and one of the driving forces in the company that bore his name. The lack of complexity and difficulty in the programme is attested by the fact that the whole project was less than 16 months old when Floyd Carlson made the

XH-40's maiden flight at Fort Worth. Already a service test batch of six YH-40 helicopters had been ordered, and while these were being built the three XH-40s undertook the preliminary flight trials and service evaluation, in which they were supplemented by the YH-40 helicopters. These had all been delivered by August 1958, and featured a lengthened cabin (demanded after further evaluation of the basic design incorporated in the XH-40 helicopters), taller skid landing gear and 770-shp (574-kW) engines. For the development programme, Bell retained the three XH-40s and one YH-40, and of the remaining YH-40s one was despatched to Eglin Air Force Base for climatic and cold-weather testing, one was allocated to

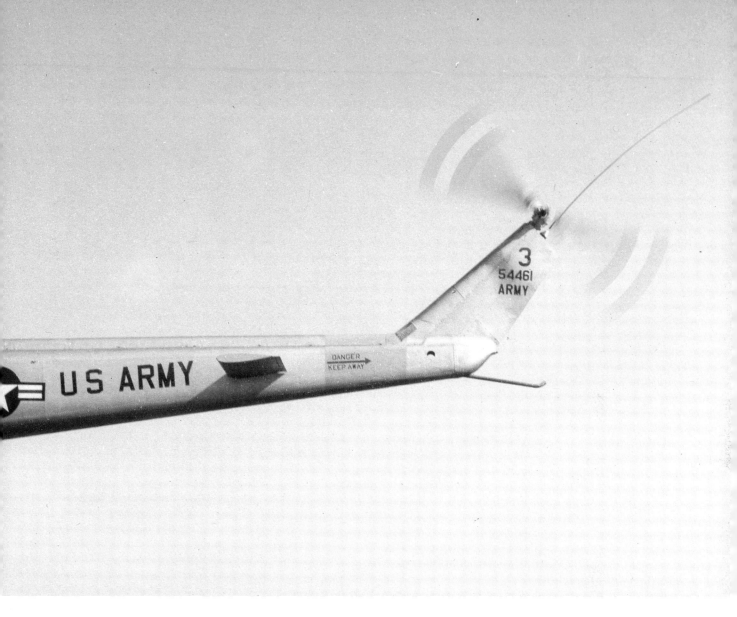

Edwards Air Force Base for US Air Force evaluation, and the remaining three were operated at Fort Rucker (home of US Army rotary-wing aviation) for a variety of US Army trials. At Fort Rucker the manifest wisdom of lengthening the fuselage by 12 in (30.5 cm) and heightening ground clearance by 4 in (10 cm) was confirmed, as were lesser changes such as a simplification of the controls and the widening of the crew doors. The increase in the length of the cabin permitted four rather than three litter patients to be accommodated.

Tests confirmed the overall suitability of the H-40 design for the US Army's specified missions, and the type was ordered into production under the basic

designation HU-1 and name Iroquois. The HU designation prefix indicates the US Army's realization that turbine power had produced a new type of capability, and this was indicated by the Helicopter Utility designator.

Above: 55-4461 was the third of three Bell XH-40 prototypes, and differed only a little from initial production machines.
Below: The YH-40 introduced a lengthened cabin, taller landing gear and revised engine/transmission accommodation.

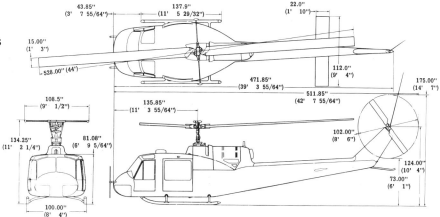

The Bell Model 204

The initial production model was the UH-1A, which was modelled closely on the YH-40 but was powered by an 860-shp (641-kW) T53-L-1A turboshaft derated to 770 shp (574 kW) for reliability and increased time between overhauls. Production of this model eventually totalled 182 examples, and much was achieved with the type in the development of operational doctrines and the gaining of operational experience. The type first served abroad in 1960-1, when examples were despatched to the Panama Canal Zone, South Korea, Alaska and Europe for evaluation under the service conditions and climates in which the US Army was most likely to find itself embroiled.

This initial production model was notable for its short rotor mast in comparison with later models, and the main rotor blades had a chord of 15 in (0.381 m). Another distinguishing feature was the location of the main-blade counterweights, which extended downwards from the blade-retention bolts. The crew was three (pilot, co-pilot and crew chief), and cabin accommodation was provided for four passengers, who entered and exited through a wide aft-sliding door in each side of the cabin. The first such UH-1As were delivered on 30 June 1959, nine initial examples being used for further development flying and 14 going to the Army Aviation School for instrument flying training.

These latter had dual controls and provision for blind-flying instrumentation as TH-1As.

Deliveries of the UH-1A were completed by March 1961, by which time the helicopter was in service with Aviation Companies and Medical Ambulance Companies of the US Army in the continental USA, the 82nd Airborne Division in Panama, the 55th Aviation Company in South Korea and comparable units in Alaska and Europe. It had been appreciated by this time that the front-line deployment of UH-1 helicopters would be much facilitated by the provision of some type of organic armament (such as unguided rockets in pods for the suppression of hostiles in proposed landing zones, and light machine-guns on flexible mountings for the elimination or at least engagement of point targets in the landing zone), and experiments along these lines were carried out in the USA during 1960.

This experience proved its value when the UH-1 was blooded in 1962, some 13 of the UH-1A model having been allocated to the Utility Tactical Transport Helicopter Company in South Vietnam. This UTTHC soon found itself embroiled in the opening phases of the USA's involvement with this unhappy region, and extemporized mountings for a pair of 0.3-in (7.62-mm) Browning machine-guns and 16-tube pods for 2.75-in (70-mm) unguided rockets were soon in evidence. Unhappy though it might have been for the USA as a whole, Vietnam was the making of the HU-1, for the type's payload capability, operational flexibility and mechanical reliability were all

proved rapidly, and the type went on to become the real 'maid of all work' in this climatic struggle. By the time the UTTHC was firmly involved in Vietnam, the basic model had changed designation as a result of the US Armed forces' tri-service designation rationalization agreement, which came into effect during October 1962. Under this revised system the HU-1 became the UH-1, though the nickname 'Huey' derived from the original US Army designator was now too firmly entrenched to be modified, and this rapidly became the name by which the whole series was and is still best known. Other nicknames proliferated, but these were peculiar to the US Army and have never received the widespread acceptance of 'Huey': typical of these names are 'Slick' for unarmed troop-carrying UH-1s and 'Hog' for armed UH-1s.

The armed UH-1As proved to be the ideal escort for UH-1As operating in other roles, the extra drag of the armament installation being balanced by the weight of the extra payload in the other helicopters so that both types had comparable performance. This meant that, as more helicopters arrived in Vietnam, types such as the Douglas B-26 Invader and North American T-28 Trojan could be freed of their landing-zone preparatory role, which was now undertaken by UH-1 'Hogs'. The UH-1 had not been designed for such a role, however, and therefore lacked a number of essential features, such as armour protection for the crew and vital systems, and as heavier weapon loads were demanded the UH-1 'Hogs' soon began to suffer from a distressing lack of performance in comparison with the UH-1 'Slicks'. However, the loss rate of the 'Slicks' declined rapidly with the development of 'Hog' models, though it was clear that operational flying had found the basic design short of power for fully-laden operations.

Left: 57-6099 was the fifth production example of the UH-1A (initially HU-1A), and is seen here in the hover with an overload fuel tank occupying the payload area of the cabin.

Above: Though based on the airframe of a Bell Model 204 helicopter, the experimental HueyTug had a much uprated dynamic system to pioneer the possibilities of the 'Huey' as a lift helicopter.

This fact had been appreciated by the US Army some time earlier, and in June 1959, the month in which the first HU-1As were delivered, the service had contracted with Bell for four YHU-1B prototypes with an uprated powerplant and other modifications. The first YHU-1B made its initial flight in April 1960, and deliveries of an eventual 1,010 to the US Army began in March 1961. Powered initially by a 960-shp (716-kW) T53-L-5 turboshaft, the UH-1B (as the HU-1B was redesignated in the 1962 designation rationalization) featured a rotor mast increased in height by 13 in (33 cm), revised rotor blades of honeycomb construction with a chord of 21 in (53 cm), and counterweights extending upwards rather than downwards as on the UH-1A.

During the production run of the UH-1B, the powerplant was successively upgraded, first to the 1,100-shp (820-kW) T53-L-9 and later to the T53-L-11 of the same power rating but with improved fuel consumption and greater reliability. The cabin was also enlarged further to provide accommodation for the crew chief and six passengers; an alternative load was three litters in a tier at the rear of the cabin, plus two sitting casualties and an attendant. The UH-1B was widely used in Vietnam with an increasingly diverse number of armament fits, both official and unofficial, and during the type's service life retrofits added armoured seats and a number of other survival features. The type is also credited with an unofficial world helicopter speed record at 222 mph (357 km/h),

though operational speeds were much lower because of the drag and weight of equipment, and the basic limitations of the wide-chord two-blade main rotor, which was also very noisy. The 'slap-slap' of an oncoming 'Huey' became a sound typical of the Vietnam War, and was at times a very distinct tactical disadvantage, permitting the Viet Cong or North Vietnamese opposition to conceal themselves before the arrival of a helicopterborne assault, and so to survive the initial suppression fire and then pop up and pour a withering fire into the helicopters at their most vulnerable in the hover or on the ground.

The UH-1C was based on the UH-1B but had the Model 540 rotor, main rotor blades of 27 in (68.58 cm) chord and an increased chord tail rotor pylon with anti-torque camber. Useful load was 4,673 lb (2120 kg).

Above: Though built for the US Army, the UH-1B was also used in limited numbers by the US Navy for Vietnam operations with the M6 armament subsystem (belt-fed fixed machine-guns and rockets carried outside the cabin) in addition to door-mounted flexible machine-guns.

Right: A heavily armed UH-1B of Light Helicopter Attack Squadron 3, Detachment 7, prepares for a sortie from Binh Thuy air base in South Vietnam during February 1968. Note the external armament fit.

Below: Many 'Hueys' were lost in Vietnam, none more poignantly than the machines such as this Vietnamese 'Huey' being jettisoned over the side of the USS *Blue Ridge* during the evacuation of Saigon in April 1975.

The UH-1B was the first of the series to receive an export order, the Royal Australian Air Force ordering eight of the type in April 1960. It was only the beginning of a glowing export and licence-production record for the 'Huey' series.

The standard armament fit of the UH-1B slowly standardized at a maximum of four 0.3-in (7.62-mm) M60 machine-guns plus two packs each containing 24 2.75-in (70-mm) unguided rockets, or roughly double what the UH-1A could carry, and the type's extra capability is reflected by the increased payload, which as an alternative to the passenger/casualty load mentioned above could comprise 3,000-lb (1361-kg) of freight carried internally or externally.

The UH-1B may be regarded as the first definitive production variant of the 'Huey', and the maturity of the basic design is confirmed by the launch of a civil version, the Model 204B powered by the 1,100-shp (820-kW) T5311A turboshaft. In comparison with the UH-1B, the Model 204B featured a main rotor with a diameter of 48 ft (14.63 m) rather than the 44 ft (13.41 m) of the military helicopter, and a tailboom lengthened by 2 ft (61 cm) to enhance directional control and also to provide the volume needed for a baggage compartment. The Model 204B was also exported in various forms to overseas military operators, and the type was also built under licence in Japan and Italy by Fuji and Agusta (see below). The most readily distinguishable feature of the model from a visual aspect was the relocation of the tail rotor from the port to the starboard side of the tail pylon.

Right: An experimental fit on the UH-1B was a group of six Nord AS.11 wire-guided anti-tank missiles, seen here in April 1962.
Inset top right: A rescue-equipped UH-1C of the Royal Norwegian air force.
Insert above: Norway's 'Hueys' are used for adverse-terrain transport and army support.
Inset far right: A Norwegian 'Huey' practises casualty-evacuation procedures.

The UH-1E has an aluminium- rather than magnesium-alloy basic structure.

The UH-1C was built in relatively small numbers as an interim gunship version for the US Army pending deliveries of the definitive AH-1G HueyCobra slim-fuselage gunship, but also served to introduce an improved rotor system, the Bell-developed Model 540 'door-hinge' type that permitted greater speed and also greater agility. Production totalled 767, and the type may be regarded as the production and operational successor to the UH-1B, which it resembled apart from its rotor system. Less obvious changes were the provision of extra fuel capacity and twin hydraulic systems to improve combat survivability. At the same time the chord of the tail pylon was increased slightly, and also given a camber to reduce the effects of main-rotor torque reaction by aerodynamic means. The new rotor also had blades increased yet further in chord, this time to 27 in (69 cm), and the UH-1C was thus able to lift a useful load of 4,673 lb (2120 kg). When fitted with the 1,400-shp (1044-kW) T53-L-13 engine the UH-1C became the UH-1M, and deliveries of the UH-1C began in June 1965, allowing the type rapidly to supplement the UH-1B during the increasingly

heavy fighting that was developing in Vietnam.

A one-off development of the UH-1C was the HueyTug, which was a UH-1C fitted with a 2,650-shp (1976-kW) T55-L-7 engine, uprated transmission and 50-ft (15.24-in) diameter 'door-hinge' main rotor. Combined with a strengthened airframe, a larger boom and an increased-diameter tail boom, the more capable dynamic system allowed the HueyTug to lift a 6,720-lb (3048-kg) payload. Other performance attainments of the model were a maximum speed of 161 mph (259 km/h) and the ability to hover out of ground effect at 4,000 ft (1525 m) at a maximum take-off weight of 14,000 lb (6350 kg). The experience with its HueyTug proved invaluable when Bell came to develop real 'lift' versions of the 'Huey' series.

The UH-1C was preceded into service by the much-altered UH-1D, the first of a developed model designated as the Model 205 by Bell and discussed below.

Thus the next version of the baseline model for the US military was the UH-1E, developed from the Model 204B for the US Marine Corps' Assault Support Helicopter requirement, issued in 1962 to find a replacement for the Cessna O-1B fixed-wing aircraft currently in service. The US Marine Corps' first

UH-1E flew in February 1963, and resembled the US Army's UH-1B in appearance apart from the housing for the specified personnel hoist on top of the cabin. Other differences were special avionics, a rotor brake and other items of US Marine Corps equipment, and a radical, though totally unobvious modification was a structure of aluminium alloy, the magnesium alloy used in previous models being horribly vulnerable to salt-water corrosion in the naval environment typical of US Marine Corps operations. Early production used the original 44 ft (13.41 m) main rotor with 21 in (53 cm) blades, but during the course of the production run for 192 UH-1Es the Model 54C rotor was adopted, this having a diameter of 48 ft (14.63 m) with blades of 27 in (69 cm) chord. Thus later-production UH-1Es had greater lifting capacity than the early helicopters with the same designation. The type entered service with Marine Air Group 26 at New River, North California in February 1964, and the UH-1E is also notable for being the first 'Huey' variant to feature an optional chin turret, the TAT-101 unit mounting two 0.3 in (7.62 mm) M60 machine-guns. The TH-1E was a trainer version of which 20 were built.

The reputation and capabilities

The Royal Australian Air Force operates some 26 Bell UH-1D/H helicopters for a number of tasks, the operator units being Nos 5 and 9 Squadrons.

Above: Bell Model 205s of the US Army in typical 'Huey' guise are seen in Vietnam with characteristic light armament.

Below: A Bell UH-1B of the US Navy's Light Helicopter Attack Squadron 3 prepares for a strike mission from Binh Thuy in 1968.

Above: The twin-engined Bell UH-1N was produced in moderate numbers for the US forces, this being one of 204 such multi-role helicopters accepted by the US Navy and US Marine Corps; twin-engine safety was much appreciated by crews.

Below: The US Marine Corps accepted 192 examples of the UH-1E, a version of the UH-1B with USMC equipment and the T53-11 turboshaft. The type was retrofitted with the broader-chord main rotor blades seen in this illustration.

Right: Seen in delivery condition, this 'Huey' is one of 767 UH-1Cs based on the UH-1B for the US Army.

Right: Key to the success of the UH-1 series was the excellent Avco Lycoming T53 turboshaft, seen here as the T53-L-13B.

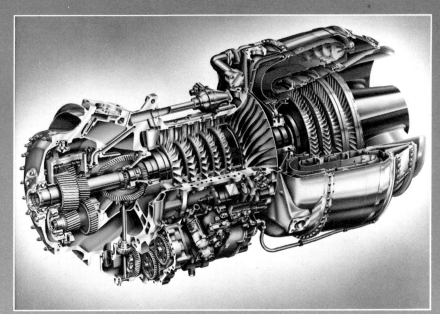

Below: The HH-1H was the base rescue variant of the Model 205 for the US Air Force, and is seen here in the form of a machine of the 1550th Flight Training Squadron before take-off from Hill Air Force Base in Utah for a rescue training sortie during 1973.

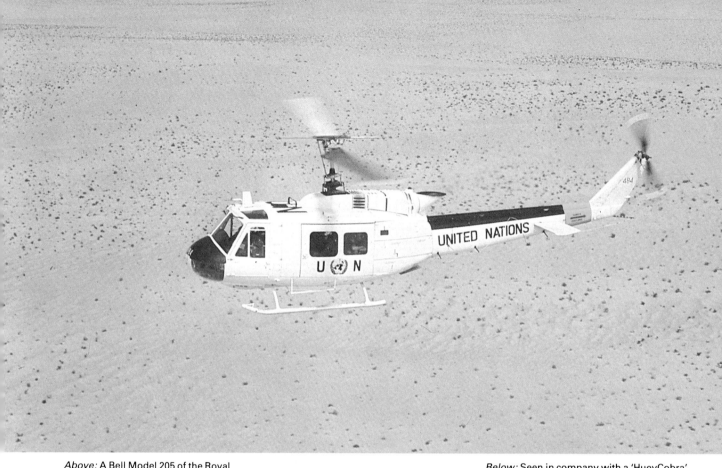

Above: A Bell Model 205 of the Royal Australian Air Force sports the highly distinctive colour scheme and markings required of UN machines in the Middle East.

Below: Seen in company with a 'HueyCobra' gunship helicopter is a UH-1E of the US Marine Corps, the type's basic Model 204 kinship being shown by the short cabin.

Above: A Bell UH-1D/H of the Royal New Zealand Air Force's No. 3 Squadron practises a rescue operation. The squadron is based at Hobsonville on North Island.

Below: One of the ultimate developments of the Model 204 basic designs is the Model 412 twin-engine machine with four-blade main rotor, seen here in Venezuelan guise.

Left: Some indication of the external lift capability of the 'Huey' series is provided by this Model 208 Huey Tug, an experimental model that did not enter production.

Above: Designed to a Canadian specification with a Canadian twin-engine powerplant, the Model 212 serves with the Canadian Armed Forces as the popular CH-135.

Below: Used by the Canadian Armed Forces for a variety of tasks, the CH-118 is the Canadian version of the UH-1H general-purpose helicopter.

of the early 'Hueys' were now attracting more customers, and this is evidenced by the next model. This was the UH-1F for the US Air Force, which in June 1963 revealed that a variant of the Model 204 had been selected as the service's new site-support helicopter. However, to ease maintenance and spares-holding problems, the USAF decreed that the new model should be powered by the same General Electric T58 turboshaft as used in its Sikorsky CH-3 helicopters, so the UH-1F was powered by a T58-GE-1, 272-shp T58-GE-3 derated to 1,100 shp (820 kW) in this application. The first UH-1F made its maiden flight on 20 February 1964, and the first operational aircraft was handed over to the 4486th Test Squadron at Eglin Air Force Base in

September 1964. Total production amounted to 120 aircraft, which had a number of commercial Model 204B features, such as the baggage comparment in the starboard side of the boom, and the main rotor was of the 48 ft (14.63 m) type with 21 in (53 cm) blades. Some of these UH-1Fs were later modified for the gunship role in Vietnam, and when fitted with an armament of one pintle-mounted 7.62-mm (0.3-in) Minigun in the cabin and 7-tube pods for 2.75-in (70-mm) unguided rockets these helicopters were redesignated UH-1P. A recognition feature of the UH-1F and UH-1P is the exhaust, which instead of being a rearward extension of the powerplant assembly as on early models is routed to emerge on the starboard side of the assembly.

The UH-1F has a T58 turboshaft exhausting to the right rather than straight aft.

From the UH-1F was developed the TH-1F, a specialized model for instrument and hoist training. Production of this variant amounted to 26 aircraft.

Next in order of suffix designations within the Model 204 family came the HH-1K. This was based on the aluminium-alloy UH-1E, but was designated for search and rescue operations with the US Navy. Production amounted to 27 aircraft and these, powered by 1,400-shp (1044-kW) T53-L-13 turboshafts, were delivered from May 1970.

The second UH-1F for the USAF is seen with an instrumented air-data probe on the nose.

The US Navy was also the customer for the last two new-build 'Huey' variants, the TH-1L and UH-1L, both powered by the 1,400-shp (1044-kW) T53-L-13 turboshaft derated to 1,100 shp (820 kW). Both models were based on the airframe of the UH-1E (aluminium-alloy construction), but had no provision for armament and were never fitted with armour protection. The UH-1L was intended for utility duties, and a total of eight were delivered in November and December 1969. The TH-1L was produced in larger numbers (90 helicopters), and these were delivered from November 1969 for use exclusively as trainers.

Mention should also be made of two converted models, the RH-2 and the UH-1M. The former was a single UH-1A modified as a flying research laboratory, and the latter comprised three conversions from UH-1Cs to evaluate under operational conditions in Vietnam the INFANT system developed by the Hughes Aircraft Company under US Army Contract. This Iroquois Night Fighter And Night

Tracker system, contracted in 1967, comprised the whole assembly of helicopter, low-light-level TV camera, and the weapons, and was designed to provide the US Army with a means of engaging an elusive enemy during the nocturnal operations that were the communists' forte. A position under the nose was selected for the LLLTV equipment, which was designed to pick up men and equipment under conditions of starlight and moonlight, so the UH-1M's M21 armament system (two 7.62 mm/0.3 in Miniguns and two 7-tube pods for 2.75 in/70 mm unguided rockets, located as a pair of each type at the ends of the armament outriggers) could be brought into effective play. A special type of dim tracer round was developed as the conventional tracer round blinded the LLLTV, and one million such rounds (used in the ratio of 1:9 with conventional ball ammunition) were produced; the M134 Miniguns were also modified with flash suppressors to avoid damaging the sensitive optics of the LLLTV. The three aircraft were

evaluated in a three-month period up to February 1970, each operating as part of a four-helicopter mission team (two gunships, one command helicopter and the INFANT) to identify and mark targets for the gunships. The UH-1M was flown as a two-seater, the pilot flying the helicopter as usual and the co-pilot operating the LLLTV system and armament system. The operating unit was the 227th Aviation Battalion, and during the course of the evaluation period this unit served with the 1st Aviation Brigade, the 1st Infantry Division and the 25th Infantry Division to secure maximum diversity of operational environments and tactics. The experiment was moderately successful, but it was felt that better capabilities were offered by fixed-wing aircraft such as the Lockheed AC-130A Hercules gunships.

Below: A Bell three-view details the primary dimensions of the UH-1E, HH-1K, TH-1L and UH-1L.
Above right: 157851 was the US Navy's first UH-1L utility helicopter.
Below right: The TH-1L is the trainer counterpart to the UH-1L in Navy service.

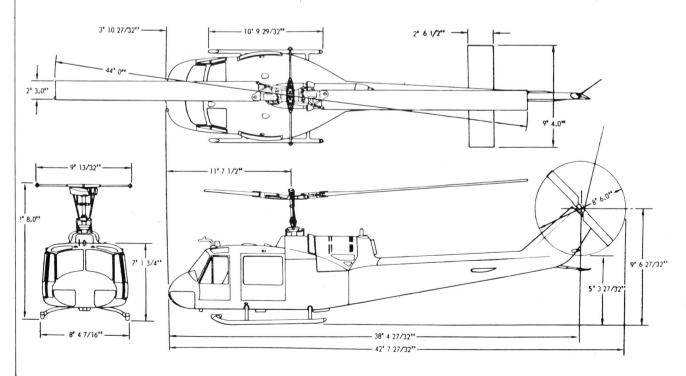

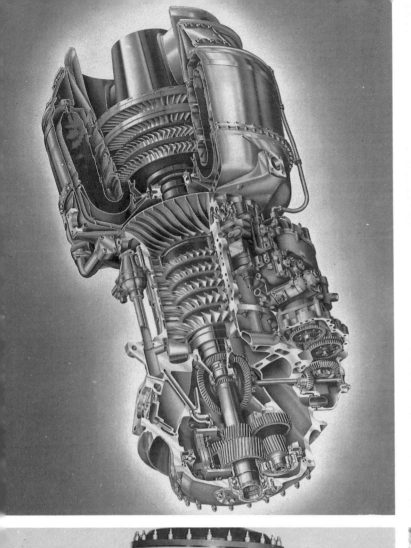

The Model 204B was also built in military and commercial variants under licence, as noted above. The principal such licensees were Agusta in Italy, and Fuji in Japan. The Italian product is generally known as the Augusta-Bell AB.204, and was produced in two main variants. The more numerous of the two models was the AB.204B, which was produced for civil and military applications between 1961 and 1974. The military examples were delivered to Austria, Ethiopia, Italy, The Netherlands, Saudi Arabia, Spain, Sweden and Turkey, though the list of operator countries is now longer as a result of resales and modification of civil craft, which were delivered to Italy, Lebanon, Norway, Sweden and Switzerland. In all essential respects the AB.204B was identical with the Model 204, and was produced with 44 ft (13.41 m) or 48 ft (14.63 m) rotors. In the powerplant, however, there was a

Above, far left: T53-L-13B cutaway view.
Above left: T53-L-13B powerplant.
Below, far left: T53-L-11 powerplant.
Below left: T58-GE-3 powerplant.
Below: The civil counterpart of the first UH-1s was the Model 204B. Few were built.

fair degree of choice, for the AB.204B was offered with the Avco Lycoming T53, the General Electric T58 and the Rolls-Royce/Bristol Gnome (a licence-built version of the T58).

The other model built by Agusta was developed in Italy as a specialized naval helicopter optimized for the anti-ship and anti-submarine roles. This was the AB.204AS, which was delivered in relatively small numbers to the Italian and Spanish navies. Two armament/sensor kits were available, the choice being decided by the desired optimization. the anti-submarine fit comprised AN/AQS-13 dunking sonar connected to an electronic suite to stabilize the helicopter during the search mode, an optional AN/APN-195 search radar and two Mk 44 lightweight acoustic-homing torpedoes. And for the anti-ship role (intended for use only against fast attack craft and the like), the kit included the AN/APN-195 search radar and two air-to-surface missiles of the Aerospatiale AS.12 type. Both models could be fitted with additional fuel tankage, a rescue hoist and flotation gear for emergency landing at sea.

The models produced in Japan by Fuji were the Fuji-Bell 204B and Fuji-Bell 204B-2, both intended for civil operation. The Fuji-Bell Model 204B was identical with the Model 204B built in the USA, and was powered by a Kawasaki-built Avco Lycoming K5311A turboshaft rated at 1,100 shp (820 kW). The Fuji-Bell 204B-2, on the other hand, was developed in Japan during 1973 as a higher-powered version of the Fuji-Bell 204B, the powerplant being a Kawasaki-built Avco Lycoming K5313B rated at 1,400 shp (1044 kW). This latter model is distinguishable from the earlier Fuji-Bell 204B by the fact that it has a tractor-type tail rotor mounted on the starboard side of the tail pylon instead of a pusher-type rotor located on the port side of the pylon. Also built in Japan were 90 helicopters based on the Fuji-Bell 204B but designated UH-1B and intended as utility types for the Japanese Ground Self-Defense Force. All of the UH-1Bs had been delivered by 1973, and in the following year some of them were modified for the trials purposes with an armament of 38 2.75-in (70-mm) unguided rockets in two 19-tube pods.

The Bell Model 205

Quite early in the development of the Model 204 series, Bell and the US Army had come to appreciate that the basic design of the helicopter was capable of considerable growth, extra airframe volume and power offering the possibility of a considerably more capable machine in terms of payload. So far as the US Army was concerned, this offered the very real advantage of nearly doubling the payload of the basic UH-1 series without the delay and funding needed for a completely new design but with all the advantages of commonality of parts and operating experience.

So was born the Bell Model 205, whose first seven examples were of the YHU-1D variant ordered by the US Army in July 1960. Considerable growth in usable cabin volume was provided by relocation of the fuel cells, and this permitted the carriage of 10 troops in addition to the crew chief and the two flightdeck crew. The 1,100-shp (820-kW) Avco

Lycoming T53-L-11 turboshaft was used, but the standard rotor diameter was increased to 48 ft (14.63 m) and blades of 21-in (53-cm) chord were fitted. The first YHU-1D flew on 16 August 1961, and deliveries to the US Army of the redesignated UH-1D began in August 1963. The UH-1D, with its much enhanced payload, soon became the US Army's most important helicopter in Vietnam, and eventual production amounted to 2,008 helicopters before the line was turned over to the improved UH-1H model. Apart from its passenger capability, the UH-1D was important for its freight-carrying capacity of some 4,000-lb (1814-kg).

The UH-1D also set a number of world helicopter records, including a climb to 6000 m (19,685 ft) in 5 minutes 51 seconds, a climb to 3000 m (9,840 ft) in 2 minutes 17 seconds, and a closed-circuit speed of 134.9 mph (217 km/h). These three records were set by US Army pilots during 1962, and serve to show how advanced the

Opposite page, top: Dornier-built UH-1Ds of the West German armed forces.
Opposite page, centre: A West German UH-1D prepares to lift an underslung load.
Opposite page, bottom: The civil Model 205A proved highly successful.
Above: 60-6030 was built as a YUH-1D but converted as the Model 208 Twin Delta experimental coupled-turboshaft machine.

UH-1D was in comparison with contemporary helicopters.

Licence production of the UH-1D was undertaken in Germany, where a team headed by Dornier produced 352 UH-1Ds for the West German army and air force.

The UH-1D was phased out of production in September 1967, when its place on the production line was taken by the much improved UH-1H. This is the most numerous type in the whole series, and was produced by combining the airframe of the UH-1D with the 1,400-shp (1044-kW) T53-L-13 turboshaft for better performance with the same payload options. As with the UH-1D, the size and relatively sedate handling characteristics of the UH-1H made it more suitable to the 'Slick' than the to the 'Hog' role, so although provision for light armament (machine-guns and rocket pods) was provided, service helicopters were almost invariably operated without weapons. The US Army's initial order for 319 UH-1H helicopters was later supplemented by an order for 914 more, and eventual production of the UH-1H was 5,435 before the line was closed in 1982. The US Army's enormous fleet of UH-1Hs was augmented additionally by the re-engining of UH-1Ds to UH-1H standard.

The type also proved popular on the export market. In 1969, for example, a licence was granted to the Aero Industry Development Center for the construction of 118 UH-1Hs in Taiwan for the Chinese Nationalist army on the island. Nine UH-1Hs were ordered as such by the Royal New Zealand Air Force, and 10 CH-118 helicopters essentially similar to the UH-1H were ordered by the Mobile Command of the Canadian Armed Forces, all of them being delivered during 1968; the original designations were CUH-1D and then CUH-1H.

Right: The Royal Australian Air Force flies UH-1D/H helicopters in support of Australian army ground operations.
Inset top: This RAAF UH-1D/H has an adaptor to turn the hot exhaust gases upwards, the standard nozzle exhausting straight aft (see main picture).
Inset right: UH-1D/H of the Royal New Zealand Air Force.

Left: Rope descent for Australian troops from an RAAF UH-1H Iroquois.
Top: CH-118 of the Canadian Armed Forces.
Above: Field refuelling for an RNZAF UH-1D/H helicopter on exercise in Australia.
Above right: The HH-1F is the USAF's base rescue variant of the UH-1H series.
Right: The capacious cabin and rescue hoist of the HH-1H are clearly visible.

Although the UH-1D/H series was built in very considerable numbers, the Model 205 design spawned relatively few military variants. This is attributable to the huge success of the type in its designated troop-carrying, utility and casualty evacuation roles, to the availability of older but nimbler Model 204 variants for the intermediate armed role, and to the development of other turbine-engined helicopters for other dedicated roles. There were three variants, however, in the form of the HH-1H, the EH-1H and the UH-1(SOTAS). The HH-1H is a US Air Force base-rescue variant of the UH-1H. Some 30 examples of the HH-1H were ordered in November 1970, and all had been delivered by the end of 1973. The EH-1H was a more adventurous development, at least one and probably more UH-1H being converted under this designation as part of the 'Project Quick Fix' programme controlled by the US Army Security Agency for the location and jamming of enemy radio communications. At the same time another UH-1H was converted into a variant whose formal designation has never been released but which is generally known as the UH-1(SOTAS). There is little hard information about 'Huey' helicopters modified for airborne radar intelligence-

gathering, but it is known that the UH-1(SOTAS) was the only operational variant of the series, and consists of a much-altered airframe with special electronics. The airframe was modified under the JUH-1 experimental programme to incorporate retractable skid landing gear, the retraction being necessary to give an unimpeded field of radar vision to the SOTAS (Stand-Off Target-Acquisition System) radar, which

has a bar antenna, visually identical with that of the SLAR (Side-Looking Airborne Radar) bar antenna of the Grumman OV-1 Mohawk under the fuselage. Funding was provided in 1975, and it is believed that four such UH-1(SOTAS) helicopters were converted for service with the US forces in West Germany. Other modifications included a heated windscreen, a new navigation system and a new autopilot, and

A UH-1D/H Iroquois of the Royal Australian Air Force's tactical support force.

the complete SOTAS equipment comprised the radar with its moving target indicator capability, a small distance measuring equipment/localizer set used to fix the helicopter's position with great accuracy, a secure data-link equipment, and a ground station fitted with the requisite data-link equipment and cathode-ray tube displays.

While the designation Model 205 was reserved for military developments, Bell allocated the designation Model 205A to commercial derivatives of the basic design. The first of these was the Model 205A-1, which replaced the Model 204B in production and proved a major commercial success as a result of its relatively low cost, good performance and capability, and operational flexibility. In its standard form the Model 205A-1 is powered by a 1,400-shp (1044-kW) Avco Lycoming T5313A turboshaft derated to 1,250 shp (932 kW) for take-off, and can accommodate a maximum of 15 persons including the pilot, with baggage accommodated (as in the Model 204B) in a special compartment in the boom. The interior of the cabin was designed for rapid transformation to suit other roles, and the Model 205A-1 can be used as a freighter for a maximum of 5,000-lb (2268-kg) of cargo, as a flying crane with a 5,000-lb (2268-kg) load, as an air ambulance for six stretcher patients plus two medical attendants, as a rescue helicopter, and as an executive transport helicopter with the cabin furnished to customer specification for a

smaller number of passengers carried in a fair degree of luxury. Optional equipment to suit these and other roles include dual controls, float landing gear, auxiliary fuel tanks, an external cargo sling, a resuce hoist, and a variety of medical equipment plus attachment points for stretchers.

A virtually identical model is built in Japan as the Fuji-Bell 205A-1 with a licence-built Kawasaki K5313A turboshaft. Some civil models have been delivered, but the bulk of production has been undertaken for the Japanese Ground Self-Defense Force, which operates the type under the designation UH-1H. Bell's Japanese licensee, it should be noted, is Mitsui & Co. Ltd, so Fuji's production is in fact sub-licensed from Mitsui.

Licence production is also undertaken in Italy, to a larger scale than that envisaged in Japan, by Agusta. Models are produced for the military market under the designation Agusta-Bell AB.205 and for the civil market under the designation Agusta-Bell AB.205A. The AB.205 is a multi-purpose type differing only in detail from the UH-1H which it resembles in having a 1,400-shp (1044-kW) T53-L-13 engine. The type is in

Offering higher capacity and performance than the Model 204, the Bell Model 205A-1 proved a considerable commercial success.

service with many armed forces in Europe, the Middle East and Africa (including Iran, Kuwait, Morocco, Saudi Arabia, Spain, Turkey, the United Arab Emirates and Zambia), and can accommodate a pilot and up to 14 troops; alternative loads are six litters and a medical attendant, or freight carried internally or externally. A wide assortment of optional equipment can be installed to increase the type's versatility: options include a cargo hook, rescue hoist, floats or skis, auxiliary fuel tanks and light armament to suit the type for the tactical role. The AB.20.

The AB.205A-1 was placed into production in 1969, and resembles the Model 205A-1 in all but minor details. The powerplant is the 1,400-shp (1044-kW) T5313B turboshaft derated to 1,250 shp (932 kW) for take-off, and accommodation is provided as standard for a pilot and 14 passengers, though freight or other payloads can be accommodated. The type can also be used as a flying crane with an external cargo hook under the fuselage centreline.

The Bell Model 212

From an early point in the development of the Model 204 and its derivatives, Bell had appreciated that one of the limitations of the basic design from a tactical and operational point of view was the use of a single engine: given such a powerplant, even the smallest mechanical failure could doom to destruction an expensive helicopter, its skilled crew and a not-inconsiderable number of men or quantity of other payload. As early as 1965, therefore, the company flew the Model 208 Twin Delta, a modified UH-1D powered by two Continental turboshafts. But the US Army and other services showed little interest at the time, and commercial operators seemed more than happy with single-engine powerplants.

But the Canadian government later in the decade realized that the vast, underpopulated and frequently hostile terrain over which their helicopter crews had to operate, often under the most adverse of weather conditions, demanded a helicopter with greater safety and reliability margins than those currently in service. This provided the stimulus for the Bell Model 212, a straight development of the Model 205 with twin-engine powerplant, the PT6T Turbo Twin Pac developed by Pratt & Whitney Aircraft of Canada. In the PT6T-3 form selected to power the CUH-1N ordered to the extent of 50 examples on 1 May 1968, the Turbo Twin Pac comprised two PT6T turboshafts couled to a combining gearbox in such a way that either or both engines could power the helicopter's dynamic system. Sensors in each engine detected any failure and automatically ran up the surviving engine to compensate for the

The Bell Model 212 Twin Two-Twelve has proved very popular for overwater use because of its twin-engine powerplant.

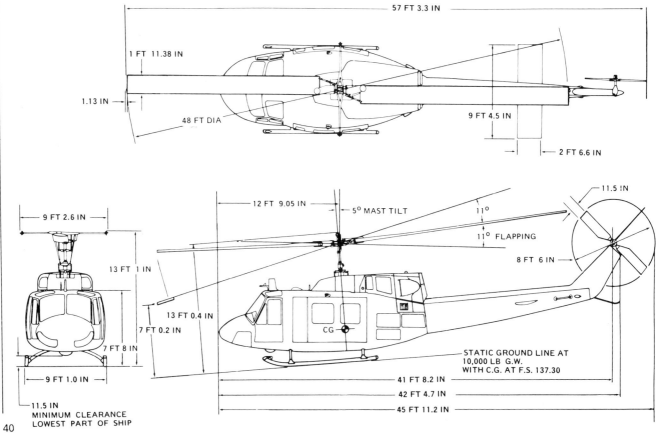

57 FT 3.3 IN

1 FT 11.38 IN

1.13 IN

48 FT DIA

9 FT 4.5 IN

2 FT 6.6 IN

9 FT 2.6 IN

13 FT 1 IN

12 FT 9.05 IN

5° MAST TILT

11°

11° FLAPPING

11.5 IN

8 FT 6 IN

13 FT 0.4 IN

7 FT 0.2 IN

7 FT 8 IN

CG

9 FT 1.0 IN

STATIC GROUND LINE AT
10,000 LB G.W.
WITH C.G. AT F.S. 137.30

41 FT 8.2 IN

42 FT 4.7 IN

45 FT 11.2 IN

11.5 IN
MINIMUM CLEARANCE
LOWEST PART OF SHIP

Left: Evolution of the Model 205 into the Model 212 was comparatively simple thanks to the overhead location of the powerplant and the pioneering work undertaken with the Model 208 Twin Delta coupled-turboshaft derivative of the UH-1D.

Below left: The basic dimensions and proportions of the UH-1N are revealed in this Bell illustration.

Below: Where the UH-1N really comes into its own is indicated by this photograph of a UH-1N of the US Navy's Antarctic Development Squadron 6 delivering a 2,000-lb (907-kg) reel of cable to a transmitter at the McMurdo Station in Antarctica.

reduction in the output of the failed unit. It was all an ingenious but thoroughly practical development, the PT6T-3 had a nominal rating of 1,800 shp (1342 kW), but was derated to 1,290 shp (962 kW) for take-off and to 1,130 shp (843 kW) for continuous running. In the event of the failure of one turboshaft, the other was capable of developing 800-shp (597-kW) of continuous power. The rotor selected for the CUH-1N (later

redesignated CH-135) was of 48 ft (14.63 m) diameter, and the blades had a chord of 23 in (0.584 m). The new model had roughly the same level of performance and payload as the UH-1H, but was clearly a far better helicopter from the operational point of view, and this was recognized by the US armed forces, who began to place large orders for the type.

First came a joint order for 141 helicopters designated UH-1N in

Above: The neat installation of the T400 coupled-turboshaft powerplant aft of the transmission and rotor assembly of the UH-1N provides good access for maintenance, and also leaves the large cabin unobstructed for payload.

Inset, left top: The extra reliability of the UH-1N's twin-engine powerplant has commended the type principally to operators with overwater and hostile-terrain requirements. Such an operator is the US Marine Corps, the helicopter illustrated being the first of the second batch ordered for the USMC and US Navy.

Inset, left centre: A UH-1N of Antarctic Development Squadron 6 is seen at Naval Air Station North Island, San Diego, before departure to the south.

Inset left: A UH-1N of the 1550th Aircrew Training and Test Wing, USAF, is seen in flight near Hill Air Force Base, Utah.

the US tri-service designation system: 79 for the US Air Force, 40 for the US Navy, and 22 for the US Marine Corps. Deliveries to the US Air Force began in 1970, and to the US Navy and US Marine Corps in 1971, these helicopters being powered by the military version of the Turbo Twin Pac designated T400-CP-400. A further 142 were delivered to the US Navy and the US Marine Corps between 1973 and 1978, but oddly enough the type failed to find favour with the US Army, whose enormous and well-tried fleet of Model 204 and Model 205 variants was deemed more than adequate for that service's requirements. Six

equivalents of the UH-1N were delivered to the air force of Bangladesh, and the sole derivative of the type in US service has been the VH-1N, a VIP transport version with luxury interior and special communications equipment. A total of eight such helicopters was received by the US Marine Corps for the VIP transport role, two being conversions from UH-1Ns and the other six new-build aircraft.

The basic type was also developed for commercial operators, and the Twin Two-Twelve (as the helicopter is designated for the non-military market) has proved a great success since its introduction in 1970. The timing was fortuitous, for it coincided roughly with the opening up of offshore resources-exploitation rigs (gas and oil) in many parts of the world, and the Twin Two-Twelve was immediately seen as an ideal support aircraft for these rigs. This tendency was emphasized in 1973 with the certification of the Twin Two-Twelve for flight under Instrument Flight Rules as well as Visual Flight Rules. A new avionics package with aircraft-stabilization capability was developed for the task, and this has allowed the Twin Two-Twelve to operate in virtually all but icing conditions, to the considerable advantage of resources-exploitation teams and companies in many parts of the world. The Twin Two-Twelve has also found favour with air-taxi companies and with large companies that require a reliable executive transport helicopter able to operate in most weather conditions.

As with earlier Bell helicopters, the Model 212 has also been built under licence and developed as a different model by Agusta in Italy. This time, however, Fuji have not come into the programme with a Japanese production capability, leaving the field to the Italian company. The baseline Italian model is the Agusta-Bell AB.212, which is modelled very closely on the American original. Like the other Agusta versions of Bell helicopters, the AB.212 is produced for civil and military operators in Europe, the Middle East and Africa, and sales have been extensive, thanks in part to the wide variety of options available on these machines. In the conventional passenger role, for example, the AB.212 can carry 14 passengers in addition to its pilot; in the air ambulance role six litters and two medical attendants can be accommodated in the cabin; and in the freighting role the AB.212 can lift an external load of 5,000-lb (2268-kg). Additional versatility is provided by the availability of float or ski landing gear, auxiliary fuel tanks and a rescue hoist.

Altogether more capable, and developed entirely by Agusta, is the potent AB.212ASW version, a multi-role naval helicopter able to undertake the anti-submarine and anti-ship roles with minimal changes to the installed electronics. The AB.212ASW has been sold to many countries (among others Greece, Iran, Italy, Peru, Spain, Syria, Turkey and Venezuela), a fact that confirms the type's true capabilities. Electronics installed in this version include Canadian Marconi AN/APN-208(V)2 doppler radar, Bendix AN/AQS-13B dunking sonar, SMA search radar, and a Canadian Marconi CMA-708B/ASW computer for the assessment of the tactical situation. The weapons that go with this electronic fit include (for the anti-submarine role) two Mk 44 or Mk 46 lightweight acoustic-homing torpedoes or a number of depth charges, or (for the anti-ship role) up to four Aérospatiale AS.12 or two Sea Killer air-to-surface missiles. These are capable of dealing with fast attack craft and the like, but for operations against large surface combatants the AB.212ASW still has a limited

though indirect part to play, as the platform for the TG-2 data-link equipment that can feed precise targeting information from the helicopter's radar to an Otomat surface-to-surface anti-ship missile fired by a warship below the horizon. Other roles that can be undertaken by the AB.212ASW, which is a truly versatile machine in the best sense of the word, include search and rescue (with a 595-lb/270-kg capacity rescue hoist) and freighting (with a 5,000-lb/2268-kg external load capacity).

Further development of the basic Model 212 design has produced the Model 412, whose development was announced by Bell in September 1978. The Model 412 is essentially the Model 212 modified to incorporate a four-blade main rotor of advanced design and construction, using

blades similar to those of the Model 214ST (see below) with a new hub system. Up to and including the Model 212, the blades were all-metal semi-rigid units built up on the basis of extruded aluminium spars and a covering. The new type of blade as used in the Model 214ST and Model 412 is based on a unidirectional glassfibre spar with a torque-laid casing of glassfibre cloth; this supports a unidirectional glassfibre trailing edge, the space between the trailing edge and spar being filled with Nomex honeycomb and the whole blade then being covered and bonded together by a glassfibre wrapping. The leading edge is protected by a titanium abrasion strip, and the tip of each interchangeable blade is protected by a replaceable stainless-steel cap.

Opposite page, top: The Italian version of the Model 212 is the Agusta-Bell AB.212, seen here in the alpine terrain in which the type excels.

Opposite page, bottom: Sporting a low-visibility camouflage scheme, a UH-1N of the USAF's 20th Special Operations Squadron practice-fires an unguided rocket.

Above: The UH-1N crews of the 20th SOS, 1st Special Operations Wing, are amongst the most highly trained in the USAF, and do much of their training in Florida.

A well-used UH-1N of the US Marine Corps is seen just before touch-down.

The development programme for the Model 412 was undertaken by a pair of Model 212s, and the type first flew in such converted form during August 1979. The Model 412 was certificated in 1981, and deliveries began during that year, since when the new helicopter has received acclaim for its low noise levels and good performance, and also for the considerably reduced vibration levels perceived in the fuselage without the need for the nodal suspension system used on a number of other Bell helicopters.

The Model 412 is also being produced in Italy by Agusta as the Agusta-Bell AB.412 Grifone (griffon), which is available in commercial, military and naval variants. The commercial version is aimed at the civilian market, and resembles the US version closely,

using the same 1,800-shp (1342-kW) Pratt & Whitney Aircraft of Canada PT6T-3B-1 Turbo Twin Pac engine. The military version is a more ambitious machine designed for roles such as tactical transport, casualty evacuation, logistical transport, patrol, search and rescue, and even limited anti-tank strike. Equipment for these diverse roles includes a self-contained navigation system to permit nap-of-the-earth flight at night or adverse daylight conditions, secure voice-communication gear and an armament fit to include a 25-mm Hughes Chain Gun cannon, high-energy rockets launched from advanced pods, and a special target-acquisition sight. In the assault and tactical transport roles the Grifone can carry 14 fully-equipped troops, and for the

logistic support role it can carry external loads up to 5,000 lb (2268 kg) in weight, items to include a jeep, mortars, components of light artillery pieces, ammunition pallets and comparable tactical adjuncts. Thought is also being given to the Grifone's use in the anti-helicopter role with four air-to-air missiles, while defence-suppression missiles are another weapon fit under investigation for this versatile helicopter. It is anticipated that the naval version of the Grifone will be comparable with the AB.212ASW, but will have more advanced sensors, and will be fitted with more advanced armament, the air-to-surface missiles being true anti-ship types able to deal effectively with moderate-size surface combatants.

Though racier in appearance than the Model 212, the Model 214ST retains its predecessor's good reliability and payload capabilities and can, when fitted with the right avionics, operate in most weather conditions.

The Bell Model 214

The last development of the 'Huey' concept, in terms of basic numerical sequence, was the Model 214 series designed to capitalize on the weight-lifting capabilities of the original Model 204 and Model 205 single-engine types. The new series began with the company-funded Model 214 Huey Plus, a development model powered by the 1,900-shp (1417-kW) Avco Lycoming T53-L-702 turboshaft to validate the concept for an advanced medium-lift helicopter put forward by the Imperial Iranian army on behalf of the Iranian government. Under the dynamic leadership of its Shah, Iran was currently upgrading its armed forces with modern equipment, and also seeking to develop wherever possible an indigenous production capability for the latest advanced transport vehicles. The Model 214 was thus seen as an ideal way for the launch and development of Iranian

Helicopter Industry, which was slated to become the country's major source of helicopters after developing its capabilities with licence production of the Model 214.

From the Model 214 was evolved the Model 214A specifically to meet the Iranian requirement, and an order for 287 of the type was announced in December 1972, the purchasing agent being the US Army on behalf of the Imperial Iranian army. The new type was based closely on the Huey Plus, but was powered by a 2,930-shp (2185-kW) Avco Lycoming LTC4B-8D turboshaft developed from the T53-L-7C engine used in earlier Model 214A pre-production helicopters. The main rotor system for the Model 214A was based on a two-blade main rotor with a diameter of 50 ft (15.24 m) and a blade chord of 33 in (0.838 m) for maximum lift. This was particularly important in meeting

the Iranian requirement, which was taxing in its 'hot-and-high' operating demands because of the nature of the terrain over which the Model 214A was intended to operate. The Model 214A was thus able to achieve a maximum level-flight sustained altitude of 29,760 ft (9070 m), a quite remarkable achievement for any helicopter.

Other key features were the use of the 2,050-shp (1529-kW) dynamic system (transmission and rotor drives) developed for the Model 309 KingCobra gunship helicopter, and the use of Bell's patented NodaMatic cabin suspension system. This latter, evolved during 1972, was a considerable breakthrough in helicopter technology, and offered the possibility of cutting down the effects of vibration induced by the main rotor to a point where cabin vibration levels were little worse than those encountered in commercial fixed-wing aircraft.

The NodaMatic concept is based on the fact that any beam subjected to vertical vibration forces will flex in a wave pattern, which will have points of no relative movement (the nodal points) at points equally spaced from the point at which the flexing is induced. The Bell NodaMatic suspension system enabled the cabin to be suspended from such points in the dynamic system support structure, with a consequent reduction in cabin vibration levels of between 70 and 90 per cent. this was particularly important for Bell's twin-rotor designs, which had hitherto been notable for their high vibration levels.

The first Model 214A for Iran was flown on 13 March 1974, and deliveries to the Imperial Iranian army started in April 1975, soon building up to the rate of 10 helicopter per month. The initial order for 287 helicopters was boosted by another six in 1977 while plans were afoot for the launch of Iranian production, initially in the form of 50 Model 214A helicopters assembled in Iran from knock-down components delivered from Bell. Service in Iran, where the helicopter was designated the Isfahan, soon confirmed all that had been hoped of this advanced type, for as an alternative to its normal load of 15 passengers, the Model 214A proved capable of lifting an external load of 15,000 lb (6804 kg) under optimum conditions. At the same time serviceability was high, and the Model 214A proved easy to handle under all flight conditions. Further proof of the type's capabilities, if any were needed, came in the form of a series of world helicopter records established by Major General Manouchehr Khosrodad, commander of the Imperial Iranian army's aviation component, with

Bell Model 214A of the Imperial Iranian army.

Bell's assistant chief production test pilot as his co-pilot. These records included the sustained-altitude mark already mentioned, and also time-to-altitude marks of 1 minute 58 seconds to 3000 m (9,840 ft), 5 minutes 13.2 seconds to 6000 m (19,685 ft) and 15 minutes 5 seconds to 9000 m (29,530 ft).

In February 1976, with deliveries of the Model 214A well under way, the Iranian government ordered 39 examples of the Model 214C, a derivative of the Model 214A optimized for the search and rescue mission. These Model 214C helicopters had all been delivered by the time the USA ceased trading with Iran in 1979 after the overthrow of the Shah, but deliveries of the Model 214A were curtailed at the 296th machine (including knock-down helicopters).

The commercial possibilities of the Model 214A were not lost on Bell, and the company in 1974 announced the Model 214B BigLifter version for the civil market. This was very similar to the Iranian military model but has commercial avionics, detail modifications and a fire-suppression system, as well as such advanced features as non-lubrication elastomeric bearing in the tail rotor and on the flap hinges of the main rotor, and automatic flight-control system (together with stability-augmentation and attitude-maintenance capability), NodaMatic cabin suspension and a powerplant deck that opens to form an inbuilt maintenance platform. The powerplant comprised a 2,930-shp (2185-kW) Avco Lycoming T5508D turboshaft flat-rated to a maximum of 2,250 shp (1678 kW) and working through a dynamic system based on that of the Model 214A but rated at a maximum of 2,050 shp (1529 kW) and at 1,850 shp (1380 kW) for continuous running. Passenger accommodation was limited to 14 by the internal dimensions of the cabin, but external cargo-carrying capability was rated at 7,000 lb (3175 kg) on a hook rated at 8,000 lb (3629 kg), and this capability was used by a number of operators for the agricultural and fire-fighting roles, in which nearly 8,000 lb (3629 kg) of chemicals or 665 Imp gal (3025 litres) of water or suppressant could be lifted respectively.

The sole derivative of the basic Model 214B was the Model 214B-1, certificated to a maximum of 12,500 lb (5670 kg) instead of 13,800 lb (6260 kg) with an internal load, though the maximum take-off weight with an external load remained the same at 16,000 lb (7257 kg) in both cases.

Finally there is the Model 214ST. This was developed initially for the new production complex of Iranian Helicopter Industry as a follow-on for the 50 planned Model 214A

Above: CH-135 helicopters of the Canadian Armed Forces come in for a troop lift exercise during military manoeuvres.

Above left: The Model 212 series has a useful lift capability, this Canadian CH-135 being seen with an underslung 105-mm (4.13-in) pack howitzer.

Left: A Bell Twin Two-Twelve is seen in typical service, fitted with floats and operating in support of offshore rigs.

helicopters, and the letter suffix to the basic designation initially stood for Stretched Twin, which gives a clear indication of the Model 214ST's relationship to the Model 214A: the fuselage was stretched in the area of the cabin to provide accommodation for a maximum of 18 passengers in addition to the pilot and co-pilot on the flightdeck, and the powerplant was changed to twin-engine configuration with adoption of two 1,625-shp (1212-kW) General Electric CT7-2A turboshafts operating through a combining gearbox to drive the two-blade main rotor and two-blade tail rotor. In the event of an engine failure, the surviving unit is designed to run at 1,725 shp (1286 kW) to ensure continued flight capability.

The prototype of the Model 214ST first flew in February 1977, and during 1978 Bell started on the manufacture of three pre-production examples. However, the whole programme was jeopardized by the overthrow of the Shah and the consequent termination of relations between the USA and the revolutionary Moslem regime in Iran, though the company then decided to press on with the development of the type

for the commercial market, the ST suffix now standing for Super Transport to indicate the company's faith in the very real capabilities of this advanced helicopter, whose production was announced in November 1979. The type was certificated for two-pilot operation under Instrument Flight Rules in 1982, and deliveries of initial production helicopters began soon afterwards. The Model 214ST has now acquired a solid reputation for its reliability and performance, and has proved particularly adept in the offshore resources, executive and air-taxi roles.

As can be seen from the technical descriptions of the UH-1 and Model 214ST, the basic concept of the 'Huey' has developed and evolved quite radically in the 30 years that it has been in existence. But though there may be no hardware in common between the original XH-40 and the latest Model 214ST, there can be no denial of the fact that the two types are conceptually related to a marked degree. It is an eloquent testimony to the far-sighted but thoroughly practical approach by the Bell design team in the early 1950s that their notion is still viable in the middle of the 1980s in a helicopter that is securing good sales. At the same time the future of the whole 'Huey' family seems assured for the immediate future, for apart from the in-production twin-engine models, the single-engine 'Hueys' are likely to remain in valuable service with the US and other forces (as well as with the civil operators) until well into the next century. Although the UH-1H and other single-engine models are being replaced for front-line assault tasks in the US forces, the 'Huey' was used operationally in this role as late as the invasion of Grenada during November 1983, and the hot spots around the world are still echoing with the 'slap-slap' of the twin-blade main rotor of this classic helicopter family.

Bell UH-1H technical description

Type: General-purpose military helicopter.

Rotor System: Two-blade all-metal main and tail rotors with interchangeable blades on each rotor; the main rotor blades are built up on the basis of an extruded aluminium spar and laminates, and the tail-rotor blades are of honeycomb construction; the standard Bell stabilizing bar is located at right-angles to and above the main rotor blades, while the feathering axis hub is underslung; there is no provision for blade-folding; both rotors are shaft-driven from the gearbox attached to the engine drive shaft, the main rotor system being designed to permit anything between 294 and 324 revolutions per minute.

Fuselage: Conventional all-metal semi-monocoque structure with two doors on each side; the two forward doors are forward-hinged to open outwards, and are jettisonable; the two rear doors are larger, and designed to slide to the rear for access to the cabin.

Tail Unit: This is mounted towards the rear of the boom projecting from the rear of the main portion of the fuselage, and comprises a swept vertical pylon for the anti-torque rotor (mounted on the port side of the pylon) and two halves of the horizontal tailplane (mounted about two-fifths of the way forward from the pylon); the tailplane halves are synchronized via a connection to the cyclic-pitch control to increase allowable movement of the centre of gravity.

Landing Gear: Tubular-skid type; ground-handling wheels can be attached to facilitate movement on the ground, and inflatable nylon flotation bags are an optional installation.

Powerplant and Fuel System: One 1,400-shp (1044-kW) Avco Lycoming T53-L-13 turboshaft mounted above the fuselage aft of the cabin and enclosed in metal cowlings; the transmission is rated at 1,100 hp (820 kW) and is installed just forward of the engine; the standard fuel capacity of 220 US gal (832 litres) is provided by a group of five interconnected rubber fuel cells on the centre of gravity aft of the cabin, and an overload capacity of 520 US gal (1968 litres) is provided by adding two 150-US gal (568-litre) internal auxiliary tanks in the cabin with the requisite interconnection with the basic fuel system.

Accommodation: The cabin has a volume of 220 cu ft (6.23 m³) and can provide accommodation for a maximum of 15 persons including the pilot; alternative loads are six litters and a medical attendant, or 3,880 lb (1759 kg) of freight; the cabin has forced-air ventilation.

Electronics and Operational Equipment/Systems: FM, UHF and VHF radios, IFF transponder, Gyromatic compass system, direction-finder set, VOR receiver, intercommunications equipment, bleed-air heater and defroster, comprehensive engine and flight instrumentation, powerplant fire-detection equipment, 30-volt 300-amp DC starter and generator, lights (navigation, landing and anti-collision, controllable searchlight), and hydraulically-boosted controls; optional equipment includes a 150,000-BTU muff heater, an external cargo hook, a rescue hoist and auxiliary fuel tanks (see above).

Armament: None.

UH-1 Iroquois variants and production summary

XH-40-BF: Three prototypes (55-4459/4461) evaluated during 1957 with the 825-shp (615-kW) Avco Lycoming XT53-L-1 turboshaft; these machines could carry five troops in the cabin and had provision for external troop pods.

YH-40-BF: Six service-test aircraft (56-6723/6728) with a fuselage stretch of 12 in (30.48 cm) and taller landing gear.

UH-1A-BF: Originally **HU-1A-BF** initial production model, of which 182 were built; the first 14 had the 700-shp (522-kW) T53-L-1A turboshaft and the other the 960-shp (716-kW) T53-L-5 turboshaft; several of these US Army helicopters were used for armament trials (rocket pods and 0.3-in/7.62-mm machine-guns), one with a 40-mm grenade-launcher being designated XH-1A-BF; the **RH-2** was a UH-1 used for research into new avionic and control systems such as an obstacle-locating radar (above the flightdeck) and an electronic control system.

Serial nos	Number	Constr. nos
57-6095/6103	9	10/18
58-2078/2093	16	19/34
58-3017/3047	31	35/65
59-1607/1716	110	66/175
60-3530/3545	16	176/191

TH-1A-BF: Designation of 14 UH-1A-BF aircraft fitted with dual controls and blind-flying instrumentation for use by the Army Aviation School.

XH-1A-BF: See UH-1A-BF.

YUH-1B-BF: Originally **YHU-1B-BF** service-test improved model based on the UH-1A-BF but with the 960-shp (716-kW) T53-L-5 turboshaft driving a main rotor with increased-chord blades; the type also had an enlarged cabin for eight troops or three litters; the four machines were later brought up to production standard.

Serial nos	Number	Constr. nos
60-3546/3549	4	192/195

UH-1B-BF: Originally **HU-1B-BF** production aircraft, of which 1,014 were received by the US Army; early production featured the T53-L-5, but later production switched to the 1,100-shp (820-kW) T53-L-11, and most aircraft had provision for light armament (rocket pods and machine-guns) for use in Vietnam.

Serial nos	Number	Constr. nos
60-3550/3619	70	196/265
61-686/803	118	266/383
62-1872/2105	234	392/625
62-4566/4605	40	626/665
62-4606/4613	8	384/391*
62-12515/12549	35	666/700
62-12550/12555	6	708/713
63-8500/8658	159	722/880
63-8659/8738	80	884/963
63-12903/12952	50	964/1013
63-12953/12955	3	881/883**
63-13086/13089	4	1014/1017***
63-13586/13593	8	1018/1025
64-13902/14100	199	1026/1224
64-14192/14201	10	cancelled

*these aircraft went to the Royal Australian Air Force with the serial numbers A2-384/391 and A2-018/025.

**these aircraft went to the Royal Australian Navy with the serial numbers N9-881/883.

***these aircraft went to the Norwegian forces with the serial numbers 086/089.

NUH-1B-BF: One aircraft (64-18261, constr. no. 2048) obtained for test purposes.

UH-1C-BF: Originally **HU-1C-BF** improved production version of the UH-1B-BF with greater fuel capacity and modified rotor; 767 were acquired by the US Army; one UH-1C was modified as the sole **HueyTug** with a 2,650-hp (1976-kW) Avco Lycoming T55-L-7 turboshaft and 50-ft (15.24-m) main rotor for a maximum take-off weight of 14,000 lb (6350 kg).

Serial nos	Number	Constr. nos
64-14101/14191	91	1225/1315
64-17621/17623	3	3101/3103*
65-9416/9564	149	1316/1464
65-12738/12744	7	1465/1471
65-12759-12764	6	3105/3110
65-12772	1	1472*
65-12846	1	3104*
65-12853/12856	4	3111/3114**
66-491/745	255	1473/1727
66-14420	1	**
66-15000/15245	246	1728/1973
66-15358	1	3115
66-15360/15361	2	3116/3117

*these aircraft went to the Royal Australian Navy with the serial numbers N9-101/103, N9-472 and N9-104.

**these aircraft went to Norway with the serial numbers 853/856 and 420.

YUH-1D-BF: Originally **YHU-1D-BF** service-test enlarged version (Model 205); cabin modified and stretched for the carriage of 12 troops or six litters; this version was powered by the 1,000-shp

(820-kW) T53-L-11, and the aircraft were later modified to full production standard.

Serial nos	Number	Constr. nos
60-6028/6034	7	701/707

UH-1D-BF: Originally **HU-1D-BF** production variant of the Model 205 design; procurement for the US Army eventually totalled 2,008 units, of which many were later upgraded to UH-1H standard with more powerful engine; the standard powerplant of the UH-1D was the 1,100-shp (820-kW) T53-L-11; a development of the UH-1D was the **Model 208 Twin Delta** test-bed for a twin-engine powerplant, the Continental XT67-T-1 combining two T72-T-2 turboshafts for a rating of 1,200 shp (895 kW) for take-off and 1,540 shp (1148 kW) for 2½-minute emergency.

Serial nos	Number	Constr. nos
62-2106/2113	8	4001/4008
62-12351/12372	22	4009/4030
63-8739/8859	121	4031/4151
63-12956/13002	47	4152/4198
64-13492/13901	410	4199/4608
65-9565/10135	571	4609/5179
65-12773/12776	4	5180/5183
65-12847/12852	6	5184/5189
65-12857/12895	39	5190/5228
66-746/1210	465	5229/5693
66-8574/8577	4	9339/9342
66-16000/16306	307	5694/6000
70-4507/4510	4	(for MAP)

CUH-1D: Initial designation for the CUH-1H.

HH-1D-BF: Designation of UH-1D-BF helicopters converted for the rescue role.

UH-1E: Originally **HU-1E** version of the UH-1B-BF for the US Marine Corps with the 1,100-shp (820-kW) T53-L-11, extra fuel capacity and a number of changes to equipment and avionics; the aircraft were later retrofitted with broader-chord main rotor blades; procurement amounted to 192 aircraft.

Serial nos	Number	Constr. nos
151266/151299	34	6001/6034
151840/151887	48	6035/6082
152416/152439	24	6083/6106
153740/153767	28	6107/6134
154750/154780	31	6135/6165
154943/154969	27	6166/6192
155337/155367	31	6193/6223
		(cancelled)

TH-1E: Crew-training derivative of the UH-1E for the US Marine Corps.

Serial nos	Number	Constr. nos
54730/54749	20	?

UH-1F-BF: Originally **XH-40A-BF** version of the UH-1B-BF (HU-1B-BF) for the US Air Force with the 1,290-shp (962-kW) General Electric T58-GE-3 turboshaft; one XH-40A-BF was ordered (63-13141) but later cancelled in favour of the UH-1F-BF series, of which 120 were delivered, with accommodation for a pilot and 10 passengers.

Serial nos	Number	Constr. nos
63-13141/13165	25	7001/7025
64-15476/15501	26	7026/7051
65-7911/7965	55	7052/7106
66-1211/1224	14	7107/7120

TH-1F-BF: Base-rescue and instrument-training version of the UH-1F-BF for the US Air Force, which received 26 of the model.

Serial nos	Number	Constr. nos
66-1225/1250	26	7301/7326

UH-1H-BF: Uprated version of the UH-1D-BF powered by the 1,400-shp (1044-kW) T53-L-13 for the US Army, which received 5,435 examples of the type; many UH-1D-BFs were brought up to UH-1H-BF standard.

Serial nos	Number	Constr. nos
66-16307/17144	838	8501/9338
67-17145/17859	715	9343/10057
67-18411/18413	3	10058/10060
67-18558/18577	20	10061/10080
67-19475/19537	63	10081/10143
68-15214/15778	565	10144/10708
68-15779/15794	16	17001/17016
68-16050/16628	579	10709/11287
69-15000/15959	960	11288/12247
69-16650/16670	21	12248/12278
69-16671/16679	9	17017/17025
69-16692/16732	41	12269/12309
70-15700/15874	175	12310/12484
70-15913/15932	20	12485/12504
70-16200/16518	319	12505/12823
71-20000/20339	340	12824/13163
72-21465/21647	183	13164/13346
73-21661/21860	200	13349/13548
73-22066/22135	70	13549/13618*
74-22295/22544	250	13619/13868
76-22651/22690	40	13869/13908

*73-22068/22071 transferred to Spain

CUH-1H: Version of the UH-1H-BF for Canada, where the local designation **CH-118** was applied.

HH-1H-BF: Base-rescue version of the UH-1H-BF for the US Air Force, which received 30 aircraft.

Serial nos	Number	Constr. nos
70-2457/2486	30	17101/17130

EH-1H-BF: Designation of at least one UH-1H converted for electronic warfare.

UH-1H/SOTAS: Designation of at least four UH-1Hs converted for stand-off target-acquisition duties.

HH-1K: Rescue helicopter for the US Navy based on the UH-1E but with the 1,100-shp (820-kW) T53-L-13, US Navy avionics and rescue gear; the US Navy accepted 27 such aircraft.

Serial nos	Number	Constr. nos
157177/157203	27	6301/6327

TH-1L: Training version of the UH-1E with the 1,100-shp (820-kW) T53-L-13 turboshaft; 90 were received by the US Navy.

Serial nos	Number	Constr. nos
157806/157850	45	6401/6445
157859/157903	45	6446/6490

UH-1L: Utility version of the TH-1L, of which eight were accepted by the US Navy.

Serial nos	Number	Constr. nos
157851/157858	8	6210/6217

UH-1M-BF: Conversions of the UH-1C-BF for night attack by the US Army in Vietnam; the model featured the Hughes INFANT sensor and armament system, and was retrofitted with the T53-L-13 engine.

UH-1N-BF: This was the production version of the twin-engine Model 212 for the US Air Force, US Navy and US Marine Corps; accommodation was provided for 14 passengers, and the powerplant was the 1,250-shp (932-kW) Pratt & Whitney Aircraft of Canada T400-CP-400 coupled turboshaft; deliveries amounted to 79 aircraft to the US Air Force and 204 aircraft to the US Navy and US Marine Corps.

Serial nos	Number	Constr. nos
68-10772/10776	5	31001/31005
69-6600/6670	71	31006/31076
69-7536/7538	3	31077/31079
158230/158259	30	31401/31430
158260/158291	32	31601/31632
158438/158452	15	cancelled
158548/158550	3	31633/31635
158555	1	31640
158558/158562	5	31643/31647
158762/158785	24	
159186/159209	24	
159680/159703	24	
159774/159777	4	
160165/160179	15	
160438/160461	24	
160619/160624	6	
160827/160838	12	

VH-1N: Staff transport version of the UH-1N for the US Marine Corps; two UH-1Ns (158277 and 158278) were converted to this configuration, and another six aircraft were built as such.

Serial nos	Number	Constr. nos
158551/158554	4	31636/31639
158556/158557	2	31641/31642

CUH-1N: Version of the UH-1N for the Canadian Armed Forces, which accepted 50 aircraft under the local designation CH-135 with the serial nos 135101/135150.

UH-1P-BF: Designation of a small number of UH-1F-BF helicopters converted for psychological warfare purposes in the Vietnam war.

Specifications

UH-1A

Type: utility helicopter

Accommodation: crew of two and five passengers or 3,000 lb (1361 kg) of freight

Armament: none carried as standard, but some were fitted with two 0.3-in (7.62-mm) machine-guns and 16 2.75-in (70-mm) rockets

Powerplant: one 860-shp (641-kW) Avco Lycoming T53-L-1A turboshaft derated to 770 shp (574 kW) with 165 Us gal (625 litres) of fuel

Performance:
  maximum speed — 152 mph (245 km/h)
  cruising speed — 120 mph (193 km/h) at sea level
  initial climb rate — 1,900 ft (579 m) per minute
  service ceiling — —
  range — 190 miles (306 km) at sea level

Weights:
  empty equipped — 3,930 lb (1783 kg)
  normal take-off — 6,000 lb (2722 kg)
  maximum take-off — 7,200 lb (3266 kg)

Dimensions:
  main rotor diameter — 44 ft 0 in (13.41 m)
  length (fuselage) — 39 ft 7.5 in (12.08 m)
  height — 10 ft 7 in (3.23 m)
  main rotor disc area — 1,520.5 sq ft (141.26 m^2)

UH-1B

Type: utility helicopter

Accommodation: crew of two and seven passengers or 3,000 lb (1361 kg) of freight

Armament: none carried as standard, but many with up to four 0.3-in (7.62-mm) machine-guns and two pods each containing 24 2.75-in (70-mm) rockets

Powerplant: (early production) one 960-shp (716-kW) Avco Lycoming T53-L-5 turboshaft or (late production) one 1,100-shp (820-kW) Avco Lycoming T53-L-9 or T53-L-11 turboshaft with 165 US gal (625 litres) of fuel

Performance:
  maximum speed — 147 mph (237 km/h)
  cruising speed — 126 mph (203 km/h)
  initial climb rate — 2,660 ft (811 m) per minute
  service ceiling — 16,900 ft (5150 m)
  range — 260 miles (418 km)

Weights:
  empty equipped — 4,369 lb (1982 kg)
  normal take-off — —
  maximum take-off — 8,500 lb (3856 kg)

Dimensions:
  main rotor diameter — 44 ft 0 in (13.41 m)
  length (fuselage) — 39 ft 7.5 in (12.08 m)
  height — 14 ft 7 in (4.44 m)
  main rotor disc area — 1,520.5 sq ft (141.26 m^2)

Model 204B

Type: utility helicopter

Accommodation: crew of two and eight passengers

Armament: none

Powerplant: one 1,100-shp (820-kW) Avco Lycoming T5311A turboshaft

Performance:
  maximum speed — —
  cruising speed — —
  initial climb rate — —
  service ceiling — —
  range — —

Weights:
  empty equipped — —
  normal take-off — —
  maximum take-off — —

Dimensions:
  main rotor diameter — 48 ft 0 in (14.63 m)
  length (fuselage) — 41 ft 7.5 in (12.69 m)
  height — —
  main rotor disc area — 1,809.6 sq ft (168.1 m^2)

UH-1C

Type: utility helicopter

Accommodation: crew of two and seven passengers

Armament: none carried as standard, but many with up to four 0.3-in (7.62-mm) machine-guns and two pods each containing 24 2.75-in (70-mm) rockets

Powerplant: one 1,100-shp (820-kW) Avco Lycoming T53-L-11 turboshaft with 243 US gal (920 litres) of fuel

Performance:
  maximum speed — 148 mph (238 km/h) at sea level
  cruising speed — 148 mph (238 km/h) at sea level
  initial climb rate — 1,400 ft (425 m) per minute
  service ceiling — 11,500 ft (3505 m)
  range — 382 miles (615 km)

Weights:
  empty equipped — 5,071 lb (2300 kg)
  normal take-off — —
  maximum take-off — 9,500 lb (4309 kg)

Dimensions:
  main rotor diameter — 44 ft 0 in (13.41 m)
  length (fuselage) — 42 ft 7 in (12.98 m)
  height — 12 ft 7.25 in (3.84 m)
  main rotor disc area — 1,520.5 sq ft (141.26 m^2)

UH-1D

Type: utility helicopter

Accommodation: crew of one and 14 passengers or 4,000 lb (1814 kg) of freight

Armament: none

Powerplant: one 1,100-shp (820-kW) Avco Lycoming T53-L-11 turboshaft with 220 US gal (832 litres) of fuel

Performance:
  maximum speed — 138 mph (222 km/h) at sea level
  cruising speed — 125 mph (201 km/h) at sea level
  initial climb rate — 2,350 ft (716 m) per minute
  service ceiling — —
  range — 315 miles (507 km)

Weights:
  empty equipped — 4,717 lb (2140 kg)
  normal take-off — 8,800 lb (3992 kg)
  maximum take-off — 9,500 lb (4309 kg)

Dimensions:
  main rotor diameter — 48 ft 0 in (14.63 m)
  length (fuselage) — 44 ft 7 in (13.59 m)
  height — 13 ft 5 in (4.08 m)
  main rotor disc area — 1,809.6 sq ft (168.1 m^2)

UH-1E

Type: assault support helicopter

Accommodation: crew of one and up to nine passengers or 4,000 lb (1814 kg) of freight

Armament: none carried as standard, but most with two 0.3-in (7.62-mm) machine-guns and two pods each containing seven or 18 2.75-in (70-mm) rockets

Powerplant: one 1,100-shp (820-kW) Avco Lycoming T53-L-11 turboshaft with 243 US gal (920 litres) of fuel

Performance:
  maximum speed — 161 mph (259 km/h) at sea level
  cruising speed — 138 mph (222 km/h) at sea level
  initial climb rate — 1,850 ft (564 m) per minute
  service ceiling — 21,000 ft (6400 m)
  range — 286 miles (460 km)

Weights:
  empty equipped — 5,055 lb (2293 kg)
  normal take-off — —
  maximum take-off — 9,500 lb (4309 kg)

Dimensions:
  main rotor diameter — 44 ft 0 in (13.41 m)
  length (fuselage) — 42 ft 7 in (12.98 m)
  height — 12 ft 7.25 in (3.84 m)
  main rotor disc area — 1,520.5 sq ft (141.26 m^2)

UH-1F

Type:	site-support helicopter
Accommodation:	crew of one and up to 10 passengers or 4,000 lb (1814 kg) of freight
Armament:	none carried as standard, but some with 0.3-in (7.62-mm) machine-guns and pods for 2.75-in (70-mm) rockets received the designation UH-1P
Powerplant:	one 1,290-shp (962-kW) General Electric T58-GE-2 turboshaft with 410 US gal (1552 litres) of fuel

Performance:
maximum speed	138 mph (222 km/h) at sea level
cruising speed	130 mph (209 km/h) at sea level
initial climb rate	—
service ceiling	—
range	380 miles (612 km)

Weights:
empty equipped	4,427 lb (2008 kg)
normal take-off	—
maximum take-off	9,000 lb (4082 kg)

Dimensions:
main rotor diameter	44 ft 0 in (13.41 m)
length (fuselage)	41 ft 7.5 in (12.69 m)
height	14 ft 7 in (4.44 m)
main rotor disc area	1,520.5 sq ft (141.26 m²)

UH-1H

Type:	utility helicopter
Accommodation:	crew of one and 14 passengers or 3,880 lb (1759 kg) of freight
Armament:	none
Powerplant:	one 1,400-shp (1044-kW) Avco Lycoming T53-L-13 turboshaft with 220 US gal (832 litres) of fuel

Performance:
maximum speed	138 mph (222 km/h) at sea level
cruising speed	138 mph (222 km/h) at sea level
initial climb rate	1,760 ft (535 m) per minute
service ceiling	19,400 ft (5910 m)
range	327 miles (526 km)

Weights:
empty equipped	4,850 lb (2200 kg)
normal take-off	—
maximum take-off	9,500 lb (4309 kg)

Dimensions:
main rotor diameter	48 ft 0 in (14.63 m)
length (fuselage)	42 ft 0 in (12.80 m)
height	14 ft 4.5 in (4.39 m)
main rotor disc area	1,809.6 sq ft (168.1 m²)

Model 205A-1

Type:	utility helicopter
Accommodation:	crew of one and 14 passengers or 5,000 lb (2268 kg) of freight
Armament:	none
Powerplant:	one 1,400-shp (1044-kW) Avco Lycoming T5313A turboshaft with 225 US gal (851 litres) of fuel

Performance:
maximum speed	150 mph (241 km/h) at sea level
cruising speed	140 mph (225 km/h) at sea level
initial climb rate	2,030 ft (620 m) per minute
service ceiling	12,700 ft (3870 m)
range	312 miles (502 km)

Weights:
empty equipped	4,760 lb (2167 kg)
normal take-off	9,500 lb (4309 kg)
maximum take-off	10,500 lb (4763 kg) with external load

Dimensions:
main rotor diameter	48 ft 0 in (14.63 m)
length (fuselage)	42 ft 0 in (12.80 m)
height	14 ft 4.5 in (4.39 m)
main rotor disc area	1,809.6 sq ft (168.1 m²)

Model 212 Twin Two-Twelve

Type:	utility helicopter
Accommodation:	crew of one and 14 passengers or 5,000 lb (2268 kg) of freight
Armament:	none
Powerplant:	one 1,290-shp (962-kW) Pratt & Whitney Aircraft of Canada PT6T-3 Turbo Twin Pac coupled turboshaft

Performance:
maximum speed	143 mph (230 km/h) at sea level
cruising speed	115 mph (185 km/h) at sea level
initial climb rate	—
service ceiling	14,200 ft (4330 m)
range	261 miles (420 km)

Weights:
empty equipped	6,070 lb (2753 kg)
normal take-off	—
maximum take-off	11,200 lb (5080 kg)

Dimensions:
main rotor diameter	48 ft 2.25 in (14.69 m) with tracking tips
length (fuselage)	42 ft 4.75 in (12.92 m)
height	14 ft 10.25 in (4.53 m)
main rotor disc area	1,824.4 sq ft (169.5 m²)

UN-1N

Type:	utility helicopter
Accommodation:	crew of one and 14 passengers or 3,383 lb (1534 kg) of freight
Armament:	none
Powerplant:	one 1,800-shp (1342-kW) Pratt & Whitney Aircraft of Canada T400-CP-400 coupled turboshaft derated to 1,290 shp (932 kW) with 215 US gal (814 litres) of fuel

Performance:
maximum speed	121 mph (195 km/h) at sea level
cruising speed	115 mph (185 km/h) at sea level
initial climb rate	1,745 ft (532 m) per minute
service ceiling	15,000 ft (4570 m)
range	284 miles (400 km)

Weights:
empty equipped	6,070 lb (2753 kg)
normal take-off	10,000 lb (4536 kg)
maximum take-off	10,500 lb (4762 kg)

Dimensions:
main rotor diameter	48 ft 2.25 in (14.69 m) with tracking tips
length (fuselage)	42 ft 4.75 in (12.92 m)
height	14 ft 10.25 in (4.53 m)
main rotor disc area	1,824.4 sq ft (169.5 m²)

AB.212 ASW

Type:	anti-submarine and anti-ship helicopter
Accommodation:	crew of three or four, plus a load of 5,000 lb (2268 kg)
Armament:	(anti-submarine) two Mk 44 or Mk 46 torpedoes, or depth charges (anti-ship), four AS.12 or comparable air-to-surface missiles
Powerplant:	one 1,875-shp (1398-kW) Pratt & Whitney Aircraft of Canada PT6T-6 Turbo Twin Pac derated to 1,290 shp (962 kW) with 179 Imp gal (815 litres) of fuel

Performance:
maximum speed	150 mph (240 km/h) at sea level
cruising speed	115 mph (185 km/h) at sea level
initial climb rate	1,600 ft (488 m) per minute
service ceiling	17,000 ft (5180 m)
range	363 miles (584 km)

Weights:
empty equipped	7,540 lb (3420 kg)
normal take-off	—
maximum take-off	11,200 lb (5080 kg)

Dimensions:
main rotor diameter	48 ft 0 in (14.63 m)
length (fuselage)	45 ft 11.25 in (14.00 m) with tail rotor
height	12 ft 10.25 in (3.92 m) to main rotor hub
main rotor disc area	1,809.6 sq ft (168.1 m²)

AB.204AS

Type: multi-role attack helicopter

Accommodation: three or four

Armament: (anti-submarine) two Mk 44 or Mk 46 torpedoes
(anti-ship) two AS.12 or comparable air-to-surface missiles

Powerplant: one 1,290-shp (962-kW) General Electric T58-GE-3 turboshaft with 155 Imp gal (705 litres) of fuel

Performance:
maximum speed —
cruising speed 104 mph (167 km/h) at sea level
initial climb rate —
service ceiling —
range 68-mile (110-km) radius for 1.66-hour sonar search patrol

Weights:
empty equipped 6,481 lb (2940 kg)
normal take-off —
maximum take-off 9,500 lb (4310 kg)

Dimensions:
main rotor diameter 48 ft 0 in (14.63 m)
length (fuselage) 41 ft 7 in (12.67 m)
height 12 ft 7.25 in (3.84 m)
main rotor disc area 1,809.6 sq ft (168.1 m^2)

AB.205

Type: general-purpose helicopter

Accommodation: crew of one and 14 passengers or freight

Armament: optional machine-guns or rocket pods as required

Powerplant: one 1,400-shp (1044-kW) Avco Lycoming T53-L-13 turboshaft derated to 1,250 shp (932 kW) with 183 Imp gal (830 litres) of fuel

Performance:
maximum speed 138 mph (222 km/h) at sea level
cruising speed 132 mph (212 km/h) at sea level
initial climb rate 1,800 ft (548 m) per minute
service ceiling —
range 360 miles (580 km)

Weights:
empty equipped 4,800 lb (2177 kg)
normal take-off 8,500 lb (3860 kg)
maximum take-off 9,500 lb (4310 kg)

Dimensions:
main rotor diameter 48 ft 0 in (14.63 m)
length (fuselage) 41 ft 11 in (12.78 m)
height 14 ft 8 in (4.48 m)
main rotor disc area 1,809.6 sq ft (168.1 m^2)

AB.205A-1

Type: utility helicopter

Accommodation: crew of one and 14 passengers or freight

Armament: none

Powerplant: one 1,400-shp (1044-kW) Avco Lycoming T5313B turboshaft derated to 1,250 shp (932 kW) with 183 Imp gal (830 litres) of fuel

Performance:
maximum speed 138 mph (222 km/h) at sea level
cruising speed 126 mph (203 km/h) at sea level
initial climb rate 2,030 ft (619 m) per minute
service ceiling —
range 331 miles (532 km)

Weights:
empty equipped 5,195 lb (2356 kg)
normal take-off 9,500 lb (4310 kg)
maximum take-off 10,500 lb (4763 kg)

Dimensions:
main rotor diameter 48 ft 0 in (14.63 m)
length (fuselage) 41 ft 11 in (12.78 m)
height 14 ft 8 in (4.48 m)
main rotor disc area 1,809.6 sq ft (168.1 m^2)

Model 214A Isfahan

Type: utility helicopter

Accommodation: crew of one and 15 passengers or freight

Armament: none

Powerplant: one 2,930-shp (2185-kW) Avco Lycoming LTC4B-8D turboshaft

Performance:
maximum speed —
cruising speed 150 mph (241 km/h) at sea level
initial climb rate 1,720 ft (525 m) per minute
service ceiling —
range 299 miles (480 km)

Weights:
empty equipped 7,450 lb (3380 kg)
normal take-off —
maximum take-off 16,000 lb (7257 kg)

Dimensions:
main rotor diameter 50 ft 0 in (15.24 m)
length (fuselage) —
height —
main rotor disc area 1,963.5 sq ft (182.4 m^2)

Model 214B BigLifter

Type: lift helicopter

Accommodation: crew of one and 14 passengers or 7,000 lb (3175 kg) of freight

Armament: none

Powerplant: one 2,930-shp (2185-kW) Avco Lycoming T5508D turboshaft

Performance:
cruising speed 161 mph (259 km/h) at sea level

Weights:
maximum take-off 16,000 lb (7257 kg)

Dimensions:
main rotor diameter 50 ft 0 in (15.24 m)
length (fuselage) —
height —
main rotor disc area 1,963.5 sq ft (182.4 m^2)

AB.412 Grifone

Type: multi-role helicopter

Accommodation: crew of one and 14 passengers or freight

Armament: many combinations are possible; see text

Powerplant: one 1,800-shp (1342-kW) Pratt & Whitney Aircraft of Canada PT6T-3B-1 Turbo Twin Pac coupled turboshaft flat-rated to 1,308 shp (975 kW) with 181 Imp gal (821 litres) of fuel

Performance:
maximum speed —
cruising speed 143 mph (230 km/h) at sea level
initial climb rate 1,450 ft (442 m) per minute
service ceiling 14,205 ft (4330 m)
range 261 miles (420 km)

Weights:
empty equipped 6,223 lb (2823 kg)
normal take-off —
maximum take-off 11,600 lb (5262 kg)

Dimensions:
main rotor diameter 46 ft 0 in (14.02 m)
length (fuselage) 45 ft 4.75 in (12.92 m)
height 14 ft 2.25 in (4.32 m)
main rotor disc area 1,662.0 sq ft (154.4 m^2)

Model 214ST

Type: utility helicopter

Accommodation: crew of two and 18 passengers or freight

Armament: none

Powerplant: two 1,625-shp (1212-kW) General Electric CT7-2A turboshafts with 362 Imp gal (1647 litres) of fuel

Performance:
maximum speed 164 mph (264 km/h) at sea level
cruising speed 159 mph (256 km/h) at 4,000 ft (1220 m)
initial climb rate 1,850 ft (564 m) per minute
service ceiling 7,000 ft (2135 m) on one engine
range 500 miles (805 km)

Weights:
empty equipped 9,450 lb (4287 kg)
normal take-off —
maximum take-off 17,500 lb (7938 kg)

Dimensions:
main rotor diameter 52 ft 0 in (15.85 m)
length (fuselage) 50 ft 0 in (15.24 m)
height 15 ft 10.5 in (4.84 m)
main rotor disc area 2,124.0 sq ft (197.3 m^2)